T0254147

Beginning Hybrid Mobile Application Development

Mahesh Panhale

Apress®

Beginning Hybrid Mobile Application Development

ISBN-13 (pbk): 978-1-4842-1315-5

ISBN-13 (electronic): 978-1-4842-1314-8

Managing Director: Welmoed Spahr
Acquisitions Editor: Celestin Suresh John
Developmental Editor: Douglas Pundick
Technical Reviewer: Chetan Natu
Editorial Board: Steve Anglin, Pramila Balan, Louise Corrigan, James DeWolf, Jonathan Gennick, Robert Hutchinson, Celestin Suresh John, Michelle Lowman, James Markham, Susan McDermott, Matthew Moodie, Jeffrey Pepper, Douglas Pundick, Ben Renow-Clarke, Gwenan Spearing
Coordinating Editor: Rita Fernando
Copy Editors: Kimberly Burton, Sharon Wilkey
Compositor: SPi Global
Indexer: SPi Global

Distributed to the book trade worldwide by Springer Science+Business Media New York, 233 Spring Street, 6th Floor, New York, NY 10013. Phone 1-800-SPRINGER, fax (201) 348-4505, e-mail orders-ny@springer-sbm.com, or visit www.springer.com. Apress Media, LLC is a California LLC and the sole member (owner) is Springer Science+Business Media Finance Inc. (SSBM Finance Inc.). SSBM Finance Inc. is a Delaware corporation.

For information on translations, please e-mail rights@apress.com, or visit www.apress.com.

Apress and friends of ED books may be purchased in bulk for academic, corporate, or promotional use. eBook versions and licenses are also available for most titles. For more information, reference our Special Bulk Sales–eBook Licensing web page at www.apress.com/bulk-sales.

Any source code or other supplementary material referenced by the author in this text is available to readers at www.apress.com. For detailed information about how to locate your book's source code, go to www.apress.com/source-code/.

This book is dedicated to my friends, family, and you.

Contents at a Glance

Contents

About the Author

Mahesh Panhale is a technology evangelist. He has a bachelor's degree in information technology from Pune University. He has over 12 years of experience in technology consulting and development. He has provided consulting and delivered training on multiple technologies to more than 300 software companies and corporate clients. He runs Bonaventure Systems, a software development firm based in Pune. He has completed more than 16 professional certifications on Microsoft technologies. He also delivers sessions and tech talks to the community as a Microsoft Certified Trainer (MCT). He has delivered sessions at multiple tech events arranged by Microsoft on topics such as Azure, cloud computing, and HTML5.

You can reach the author at mahesh.panhale@gmail.com for queries.

About the Technical Reviewer

Chetan Natu works as an independent consultant and trainer on Java, Android, Hadoop, and mobile applications. He has worked in various roles in the information technology field, including as a practice head over the last two decades. His primary area of expertise is in enterprise application development using Java EE, with special emphasis on UI frameworks. Chetan has also designed courses for SEED Infotech and coauthored two books on Java and Android.

Acknowledgments

Without a doubt, this book required a lot of research, discussions, and input from many helping hands. I would like to take this opportunity to mention those who made this book possible. I would like to thank those helping hands here.

In particular, thanks to Amit and Kavita Bachal for their support throughout the book writing and for the artwork.

I would like to thank helping hands Kabir Bhosale, Deepali Kamatkar, and Narendra Barhate from SEED Management Services, for making the case study work possible. Thanks to Vishal Jagtap, Rahul Kale, Mayur Tendulkar, Amod, and Latika Gokhale for their help in several topics on mobile application development.

Thanks to Prithvi Deewanji and Padmini Joshi for a lot of friendly help in technical writing.

Thanks to the technical reviewer of the book, Chetan Natu, and developmental editor Douglas Pundick for confirming the accuracy of the book's contents. Their efforts made this book tested and practical.

I would like thank to Celestin Suresh John and Rita Fernando from Apress. You made this book possible in time. It's very hard to get a book written from somebody.

Finally, I would like to give big thanks to my wife, Mugdha; my parents, MaJi; and my friends and family for putting up with this overexcited technology evangelist turned author.

What Is in This Book

This book is organized in such a way that a complete beginner will be able to develop the mobile applications. Following is the list of the chapters and a brief synopsis of their content:

Chapter 1, Introduction to Mobile Application Development Ecosystems: This chapter covers important history and trends in mobile application development.

Chapter 2, Native vs. Hybrid Mobile Applications: This chapter compares hybrid and native mobile application development.

Chapter 3, Building Blocks of HMAD: This is the most important chapter in the book. This chapter covers HTML5, CSS, jQuery, JSON vs. XML, and the basics required later in the book.

Chapter 4, Creating Your First Hybrid Application: This chapter takes you through the process of creating your first hybrid application.

Chapter 5, HMAD Internals: This application explains how hybrid applications work on various platforms.

Chapter 6, Data Access in HMAD: This chapter discusses the best practices and approaches followed for mobile application development.

Chapter 7, UI for HMAD: This chapter teaches the important 12-column grid concept from a responsive CSS type of framework such as Bootstrap.

Chapter 8, Using Device Features in HMAD: This chapter tells you how to use geolocation, a camera, and SD card features in hybrid applications.

Chapter 9, How to Advertise with HMAD: This chapter helps you understand what is required to earn money through mobile application development. This chapter explains the advertisement frameworks available and how to use the popular ones.

Chapter 10, Working with Third-Party Services in HMAD: This chapter covers the features available through third parties such as Captcha along with Open ID authentication.

Chapter 11: Setup and Deployment: This chapter explains the steps needed to created a store-based application.

Chapter 12: Xamarin vs. HMAD: This chapter explains the basic differences between hybrid and Xamarin-based applications.

Chapter 13, Case Study: A Practical Approach: This chapter guides you through developing feedback application.

CHAPTER 1

■ ■ ■

Introduction to Mobile Application Development Ecosystems

Objectives of this chapter:

- The evolution of mobile application development

- Different ecosystems: Apple, Google, Microsoft

- Problems with ecosystem-based applications

- Hybrid mobile applications

- Front-end and back-end development

- Testing of mobile applications

Today mobile device users prefer to use applications installed on their smartphones. They use installed applications (apps) for carrying out routine activities like booking cabs, buying movie tickets, and watching videos on YouTube.

This trend is confirmed by Gartner, which has this to say: "Enterprises are finding that they need to support multiple platforms, especially as the BYOD [bring your own device] trend gains momentum." (See `www.gartner.com/newsroom/id/2324917`.)

In addition, the *app-only* trend, set by e-commerce companies like Flipkart and Myntra indirectly supports this BYOD trend. App-only means that an application, which used to be available through a desktop web browser as well as a mobile device, stops operation of the web application, forcing the customer to access the application through a mobile app only.

The market share of mobile devices is divided mainly into Android, iOS, and Windows Phone. Because of the differences in platforms/operating systems, creating an installable mobile application that targets multiple device platforms requires too much of effort and expertise. For example, you have to write code in Java for Android, in Objective C for iOS, and in .NET for the Windows Phone. Shortcomings of this development approach are as follows:

- More development time

- Different expertise required per platform

- Considerably high cost of development

This can be overcome by using hybrid mobile applications, a solution based on HTML 5, JQuery, and CSS 3. These hybrid applications are created once, but after packaging can be deployed on multiple mobile devices such as Android, iOS, and Windows Phone.

1

This kind of application development has an edge over "native" application development. A Gartner survey has predicted that by 2016, more than 50 percent of mobile apps deployed will be hybrid.

Key benefits of this development approach are as follows:

- Less development effort

- Lower cost

- Common set of technical expertise required

Development of mobile-based applications depends on many factors, including the features available on the mobile device itself. One of the key parameters to consider in development is the OS platform and available screen sizes on devices.

History of Mobile Application Development

How did mobile application development (ecosystems) evolve? Let's briefly review the timeline. Figure 1-1 shows how a mobile application development process evolved over time.

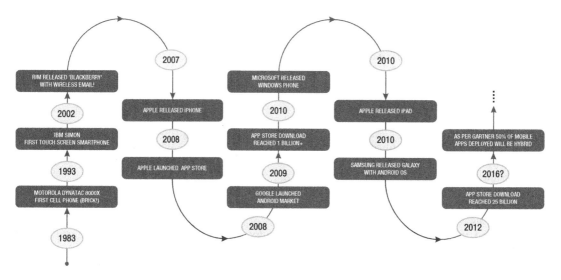

Figure 1-1. *The evolution of mobile application development*

In 1983 came the Motorola DynaTAC 8000X cell phone—the first commercial cell phone. People called it a *brick* because of its 2.5 pound weight! It was sold at the price of $3,995! This phone could do little more than calling.

The first innovations came from Nokia and other manufacturers who took this technology to another level by adding more functionality, including games such as Snake and Ping Pong. In the 1980s and '90s, mobile users had few offerings to choose from device vendors. Mobile applications were limited to those preinstalled by vendors. However, some vendors did offer applications using the Wireless Application Protocol (WAP). These applications were available from the phone manufacturers.

In November 1993, IBM launched Simon It had preinstalled applications such as a calendar, a clock, a calculator, a notepad, and email. It also had a stylus!

In 2002, Research In Motion Limited (RIM), now BlackBerry Limited, released its first device with integrated phone functionality. The product line eventually evolved into the first mass-market smartphone optimized for wireless e-mail. Mobile device users still had to wait until 2007 for a revolutionary change!

In 2007, Apple released the first iPhone, followed by the App Store launch. Users now had lot of choices for installing applications easily. A few months later, this was followed by the launch of the Android Market by Google, and the first Android-based smartphone from HTC called HTC Dream.

Apple offered its first iPad in 2010, giving users the option to use apps from their App Store. In the same year, Samsung launched a tablet named Galaxy based on the Android OS.

Understanding Ecosystems

Before proceeding, let's try to understand the ecosystems of mobile application development. To make things simple, this section introduces the three giant vendors/manufacturers in this space: Apple, Google, and Microsoft.

When a client targets a particular audience for a mobile application, how do you decide which vendor or platform to go with? This depends on multiple factors, ranging from region, location, language, domain, features required, delivery time, development team, and many more.

The Apple Ecosystem

Imagine that a client chooses a range of Apple devices for deploying an application. The Apple platform is a big ecosystem. As you may know, the iPhone, iPad, and MacBook all fall under the Apple ecosystem. These devices benefit from being in the same ecosystem, as a single store distributes iOS-based applications. Apple verifies applications and grants permission for sale based on its guidelines for acceptance.

Apple also promotes development of applications targeting the Apple ecosystem, by offering many common APIs and a common approval process. Development is made easy by Objective C and the Xcode IDE, along with many APIs to natively access (meaning at the device level) features in the app such as a camera and location.

If the application is a paid one, the revenue-sharing equation is commonly at a 30:70 ratio; Apple takes 30% of the revenue, and the application owner takes 70%. Even if the application cost includes charges paid to a service vendor such as SMS gateways, Apple still charges 30% of the total. But in any case, the Apple platform is one way for application developers to earn good revenue.

The Google Ecosystem

Let's say the same client needs to target the Google ecosystem. Do we need changes in the application? Can we port the application as it is? Are certification guidelines for Google the same as for Apple? Is the revenue-sharing equation the same?

The short answer is no. The key thing to understand is that the Google ecosystem is different. You will have to consider Android-based devices. The Android OS is an open platform to manufacturers, so the market has many device manufactures compared to Apple. Because Android is allowed to customize, this only boosts the variety of available Android devices.

Because of the multiple device manufacturers, ultimately many devices vary in size, resolution, and available features, so this ecosystem has many challenges compared to Apple. For example, if you develop an application for a Samsung Galaxy Android-based phone, changes may be required if the application is ported to a Google Nexus device, because of resolution differences.

The good point in favor of Android is that unlike Apple, application development for Android- based devices is mostly in Java. This is one of the popular and older languages, so it is easy to find programmers in Java for Android, compared to Objective C or Xcode for Apple.

The Microsoft Ecosystem

The Microsoft ecosystem is similar to that of Apple. While working in the Microsoft ecosystem, you have to consider a range of devices, including the Windows desktop, Windows Phone, and Surface. Development platforms are the .NET Framework and XNA. Microsoft has the Windows App Store for distributing applications. The preferred IDE is Microsoft Visual Studio. Mainly C# and VB.NET are the languages used for development. The process and ratio of sharing benefits remains the same as that of Apple (70:30, in favor of the application owner).

Ecosystems Are Growing

These ecosystems don't stop at phone or tablet devices. Many additions are occurring daily. Although this book focuses on mobile application development, today's ecosystems also have new additions with devices such as TVs, wearable computers like Apple watches, and more. For those who are targeting these ecoystems, development is more complex Can't we put all these devices under one giant umbrella or common ecosystem? That way, an application developed for iPhone could be easily ported to Android and also to a Windows phone.

As we discussed, developing applications around an ecosystem has benefits, such as native API availability and easy portability on devices within the ecosystem. That common ecosystem concept will need to be compromised when developing cross-ecosystem applications.

■ **Web-view application**   An application running under a web browser's context. These kinds of applications seem to be working inside the browser, but without browser windows visible.

Web Sites and Web Views for Mobile Devices

Browsing web sites on mobile-based browsers is common nowadays. Web-site development has made a few terms popular, including *front-end* and *back-end* development.

For web developers, front-end development means designing the user interface (UI) for web sites. Back-end development means coding behind the UI, and authoring code on the server side by using ASP/JSP/PHP pages.

When you develop these pages for normal desktop-based browsers, you have the liberty of using huge real estate in terms of screen size. When the same pages are viewed or browsed with mobile-based browsers, limitations related to the smaller screen size become the first obstacle.

How many people really browse web pages on mobile devices? According to Internet.org, "As of October 2014, 55% of cell phone users browse the Web on their devices." This is a huge segment that needs to be catered to.

How do you tackle the question of screen real estate? Responsive design of web pages, which resizes the UI based on the real estate (the screen size), becomes the solution. Today, CSS frameworks such as Bootstrap and Foundation provide CSS classes to design and develop responsive web sites. Web-site pages are rendered as the UI in a mobile browser. This web view can be common to many devices.

Adding JavaScript to the Mix

The browser, apart from HTML, can also understand one scripting language: JavaScript! What if a browser-based web view can be given knowledge about how to deal with native APIs and access device features through JavaScript? The web view, along with some code, can then compete with company-specific ecosystems such as Apple, Google, or Microsoft.

Can HTML-, JavaScript-, and CSS-based installable applications packaged for a particular device or manufacturer replace individual ecosystems? Can we package HTML, JavaScript, and CSS?

Partially, yes! This type of development is called *hybrid application development*.

Hybrid application development can be that larger common ecosystem that we talked about earlier in this chapter. Is it going to be limited to mobile devices only? No. This can be further extended to work with devices like TVs and watches. However, this book focuses on mobile applications only.

Will we get support from ecosystem vendors such as Apple, Google, and Microsoft? Because it's a web view packaged as an application, there is no problem. The only challenge will be extending JavaScript APIs to talk to devices.

Hybrid Application Frameworks

As you know, JavaScript executes in the context of the browser, so how can JavaScript talk to devices?

Hybrid application frameworks such as Icenium, Ionic, and Angular UI can make JavaScript capable of communicating with common devices, in a common way through one common engine or library called Apache Cordova. Hybrid and non-native application development in this common ecosystem may have to compromise in terms of the number of APIs available.

When you decide to define a hybrid application for multiple devices (including Apple, Android, and Microsoft), to get the application certified, you still have to follow norms conveyed by each vendor/manufacturer!

However, the Icenium, Ionic, and Angular frameworks do provide APIs that enable you to create common components with a common UI.

Challenges by Mobile Application Layers

Let's discuss challenges and solutions by application layers.

Front-End Development

When considering the front end in web technologies, one term promptly comes to mind: UI design. However, the front end is much more than only the UI. You have two separate and confusing terms to understand:

- User experience (UX)

- User interface (UI)

UX is not UI. Let's take a simple example from web technologies. Your client wants to have a logo—an image—at the top of the home page. Where will you put it? If you are from Asia, based on your experience, you may place it at the top left. But it depends. Who can best solve this problem is a UX -er, also known as the client's advocate.

-

UX experts are always confused with UI designers. UX-ers are not UI designers! For example, while defining native ecosystem-specific mobile applications, UX-ers are better at identifying the following:

- What customers really want in the interface

- How to provide a better experience on the small screen

- Based on the ecosystem, how the application can achieve certification

- Where to put which component

- Aesthetic structure and color scheme

A UI designer might design the interface based on the UX-er's inputs. When considering ecosystem-specific mobile applications, such as Apple and Android, the design principles differ, as shown in Table 1-1.

Table 1-1. *Apple vs. Google/Android Guidelines*

Apple Guidelines	Google / Android Guidelines
Aesthetic Integrity This represents how well an application appears. For example, in healthcare applications, the response time matters and more than the graphics. **Consistency** This confirms whether a prior user of the Apple ecosystem can use your application without any extra learning curve. Further it can confirm the following: • Is the application consistent in looking like other applications? Does it use system-provided icons and controls correctly? • Do the same icons do the thing that they are supposed to? • Is it consistent with earlier versions, if any? The following image shows consistency in terms of visual components.	**Accessibility** This ensures that the application can be used by a user with disabilities. This principle recommends including alternative approaches when a user needs to run the application under the following conditions: • Without sound • Without color • With high-contrast mode • With the screen magnified • With a combination The following shows an example of providing accessibility.

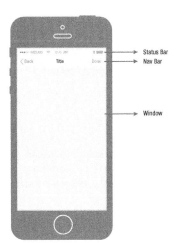

(continued)

Table 1-1. (*continued*)

Apple Guidelines	Google / Android Guidelines
Direct Manipulation In iOS applications, people expect specific results from specific gestures. The following images show gestures used for direct manipulation. For example, people can use pinch to zoom in and out.	**Navigation** Make the application easy to navigate. Show important information first. Maintain the context while the user navigates back and forth. Make sure targets can be touched by fingertips. This can be assured by making the target (may be images) at least 48 × 48 pixels. For example, if there is a Create button, place it on top, as shown here.

SMARTPHONE INTERACTION GESTURES

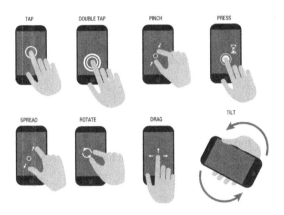

Feedback
Users should be given feedback on their actions, either through a result of the action or a progress bar.

User Control
People should initiate and control actions. If decision making is required, do not take it away from the user. In the following image, the application takes the user's opinion about sharing a location.

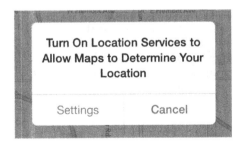

Readability
Use larger font sizes to ensure that your app is usable. Ensure that critical text has enough contrast, as shown in the following image. Give visual alternatives to sound.

Feedback
The user should be given feedback on actions via a result of the action or a progress bar.

UX - UI Problem

Because these guidelines are checked when the application receives a certificate from the ecosystem vendor, using the same user interface for many ecosystems is not possible in native application development. Note that *native application* in this context means one specific to a particular ecosystem.

Solution

Can you use a UI designed for one ecosystem as it is in another ecosystem? The short answer is no, due to the guidelines. However, for web browsers on mobile devices, the same guideline is used across ecosystems. You don't want to develop a web site or web application, but an installable mobile application.

Then why not package the web site/UI along with the code as an installable application—that is, as a hybrid application? Cross-browser issues may arise, because of the browser hosting the application or because the application is running in the browser's context. However, these issues are standard and may require less time to solve compared to redesigning the entire application for another ecosystem!

So, hybrid mobile application can be a solution here.

Back-End Development

Back-end development is again a complex term. On the Web, the *back end* refers to the code that may communicate with a server. In a mobile application development scenario, this term can have multiple meanings. Code that you write in a mobile application may do any of the following:

- Bind data with the UI(manipulate UI components)
- Get data from the UI
- Send and receive data to and from server
- Communicate with APIs offered by the ecosystems to access sensors
- Execute only business logic without a UI (for example, a service without a UI)

This functionality can be achieved by a mix of middleware components as well as including mobile app servers via Mobile Backend as a Service (MBaaS).

Sharing Back-End Code

Can you share the back-end code across ecosystems? If you are going to create a native application for an ecosystem, the language used for coding differs from that used in other ecosystems. So most of the code needs to be rewritten per ecosystem.

However, if the main business logic can be ported with service-oriented architecture (SOA), such as web services or WCF services, the logic can be reused for cross-platform and cross-ecosystem communication.

In an SOA approach as well, the logic to consume services may differ. So, the problem continues.

Solution

In hybrid mobile applications, most of the preceding code functionalities can be achieved by writing code in a single language, such as JavaScript.

In hybrid applications as well, a common business can be created as a SOA, the same as for native apps. Calling SOA inside the JavaScript code can be easy through AJAX calls, whereby you can have a choice of using the data format as XML/JSON.

8

Multiple JavaScript-based frameworks and libraries are available for achieving most of the code functionalities listed. One of the popular libraries based on JavaScript is JQuery. Hybrid application frameworks help JavaScript to communicate with native APIs, as shown in Figure 1-2.

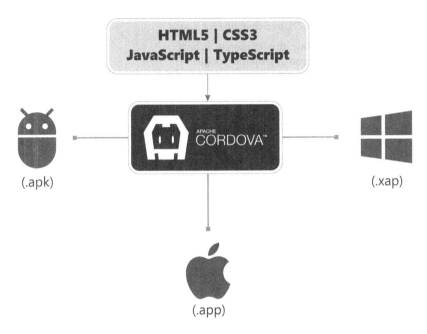

Figure 1-2. *Hybrid application with Cordova*

System Software

Many components are required to develop an ecosystem-based mobile application, including an IDE, debuggers, emulators, and packaging tools. This section provides details about the tools required for ecosystem-based applications. Table 1-2 shows Android ecosystem tools, Table 1-3 shows Apple ecosystem tools, and Table 1-4 shows Microsoft ecosystem tools.

Table 1-2. *Android Ecosystem Tools*

Language used	Java. C or C++ can be used for a few component development scenarios.
IDE	Preferred IDE is Android Studio.
Debugger	Android Studio's built-in debugger.
Packaging format	APK. Distribution is through Google Marketplace, as well as directly. Putting an app in the App Store requires approval from Google.
Development tool cost	Free
Emulator available	Yes

9

Table 1-3. *Apple Ecosystem Tools*

Language used	Objective C
IDE	Xcode IDE
Debugger	Available with iPhone SDK and installed for Xcode
Packaging format	Packaging through Xcode, distribution is through App Store only. Putting an app on the Google marketplace requires approval from Apple.
Development tool cost	Free on Intel-based Macintosh
Emulator available	Yes

Table 1-4. *Microsoft Ecosystem Tools*

Language used	C#, VB.NET, C, C++
IDE	Visual Studio
Debugger	Built-in debugger with Visual Studio
Packaging format	XAP. Distribution through Microsoft marketplace
Development tool cost	Visual Studio 2015 community edition is free
Emulator available	Yes

These tools are for building ecosystem-specific (native) applications. For hybrid mobile application development, you have many options and frameworks, such as these:

- Ionic
- PhoneGap
- Icenium
- Kendo UI
- Angular UI
- Sencha Touch
- Intel XDK

From this list, a few frameworks are freely available. Recently, Microsoft also launched a universal and mobile application project template, along with Android and iOS project templates, in Visual Studio 2015 to support hybrid applications using .NET (see Figure 1-3).

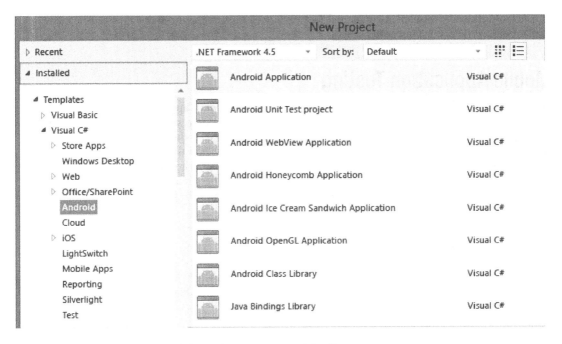

Figure 1-3. *New template for mobile applications in Visual Studio*

A company called Xamarin also did the same: the application needs to be created using .NET. Xamarin plug-in support is also added for Visual Studio (see Figure 1-4).

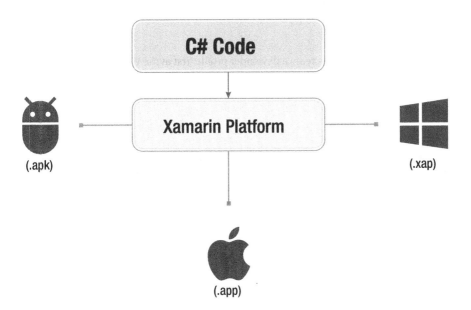

Figure 1-4. *Xamarin support*

At the Worldwide Developers Conference (WWDC) 2015, Apple announced that Swift will be made available for hybrid application development.

Mobile Application Testing

Testing is an important phase of mobile application development. Mobile applications are initially tested with emulators. However, emulators have certain drawbacks—for example, you cannot test gestures such as a pinch. Because the emulator is a program used to test the application, code for accessing sensors cannot be tested in the same manner. You can use emulators to check mainly how the user interface will look on a particular device, whether the user interface remains within a boundary when the device rotates, how the UI behaves when a different screen size is used, and so on. If you need to test the gestures and sensors, testing on the actual device is required. In this case, we are talking about testing the features of the devices and not the application code testing.

Android Testing

To test an app for Android devices, you can copy the program's output files (APK) directly onto the Android device and install it. To create a profile and upload applications to Google Play, you need to get a developer license at a cost of about $25 from Google.

Apple Testing

To test a program for Apple devices, you can create a developer profile first at the Apple app store for $99 a year. With the same profile, you can install and test applications on an iPhone. Registering 100 devices per product family is a cut-off limit for single developer profile.

Microsoft Testing

To test a program for a Windows Phone, you can create a developer profile first at the Windows marketplace, which costs $19 for an individual, and $99 for a company. With the same profile, you can install and test an application on a Windows phone.

Hybrid Testing

For hybrid mobile application testing, you can run the application as a web view inside the browser. To test the application's look and feel on different screen sizes, you can use sites such as www.responsinator.com. After testing the UI look and feel, you can test the program against sensors or on specific features by installing the application on the device itself. But even installing this application on the device requires a license in the Apple and Microsoft ecosystems. Deploying these applications on the stores requires having a profile on the stores.

Summary

A mobile application development ecosystem is a virtual environment that supports development, deployment, and testing of mobile applications.

Application development can be categorized into front end and back end. Each category has its own challenges based on the specific guidelines of the vendor or ecosystem. Ecosystem vendors such as Apple, Google, and Microsoft help developers by providing various APIs for building applications, app stores for promotions, and a platform for consistency within the ecosystem. This type of development requires you to learn a specific language and tool.

Hybrid mobile application development can target a larger ecosystem, which can consist of devices from many vendor-specific ecosystems. This type of development requires you to learn a common language and tool. Each mobile application development approach has advantages and limitations.

You will explore more in the next chapter.

CHAPTER 2

Native vs. Hybrid Mobile Applications

Objectives of this chapter:

- Understand the types of mobile application development
- Know the types and history of native mobile app development
- Know the types and history of hybrid mobile app development
- Know the commonly used frameworks for HMAD

Let's get started by understanding different ways to develop mobile applications. There are three ways to build a mobile application:

- Native mobile application development (NMAD)
- Web mobile application development
- Hybrid mobile application development (HMAD)

For the remainder of this book, we will not be focusing on the web application part, because it operates from the point of view of building an application on the Web and using the mobile device just as a front end. We will keep the discussion limited to the other two types. Let's start with native mobile application development.

Native Mobile Application Development

In *native mobile application development* (NMAD), mobile applications are developed using languages supported by the mobile OS technology stack. Before Nokia started the mobile application trend, cell phones could do only two things: make calls and send text. When a mobile application is created using the mobile OS technology stack exclusively, it is called a *native application*. These applications are built by using only the tools and technologies (including programming languages) suggested by the mobile application stack vendors, such as Google (Android), Apple (iOS), and Microsoft (Windows Phone).

History

Mobile devices have been in existence since 1973, when Martin Cooper of Motorola made the first cell-phone call to Joel Engel of Bell Labs. But for many years, the only benefit of such a device was that it allowed a person to be mobile while making the phone call. Starting in 1993, Short Message Service (SMS) was added to the device.

Serious work on making the device a personal tool (rather than a phone) for a user started back in 1996, when the Palm OS was released for a personal digital assistant (PDA). Application development for the Palm OS was more like Windows programming, which included events and loops. Applications used to be driven by a user's actions. Application development used to happen in C. The Palm OS is now the Garnet OS. Some applications such as the calculator, date book, and notepad were famous on the Palm OS.

In 1996, Microsoft launched Windows Embedded Compact (Windows CE). It was made as a plain vanilla system, and flavors were created for the Pocket PC and later for Windows Mobile. Microsoft in 2010 launched Windows Phone 7 with a tile-based UI. Application development for Windows CE used to happen using Visual Basic and C++. Windows Phone prefers development with C#, VB.NET, and Extensible Application Markup Language (XAML). The latest edition of Windows Phone (version 10) was launched by Microsoft in 2015.

After Palm OS and Windows CE, Symbian became one of the most popular mobile operating systems in the last decade. Owned by the Symbian Foundation, it was licensed by Nokia. Symbian was a favorite of developers because of its Series 60 User Interface, a software development platform for Symbian smartphones. Developers used to code in Java, C++, Python, and Adobe Flash to create Symbian applications. In 2011, Nokia declared the Windows Phone OS as its primary OS, pushing Symbian aside.

In 1999, Sun Microsystems created a Java-flavored platform called Java 2 Platform, Micro Edition (J2ME) for small devices including cell phones. Java was the obvious choice for application development.

BlackBerry launched the 850 device in 1999 and has had a variety of devices to date. It is more popular in corporate environments because of its secure e-mail functionality. BlackBerry development moves around C++ and the BlackBerry SDK.

The current market and application scenario has changed. Now the market is moved by three popular ecosystems: Google, Apple, and Microsoft. Just like the old platforms, the current popular platforms also have preferred language stacks for application development. Android has Java, iOS has Objective C, and Windows Phone has C# and VB.NET.

To summarize, the following are important milestones in mobile history:

- 1973 DynaTAC mobile phone by Motorola

- 1995 IBM Simon has a touch screen, e-mail, and PDA features

- 1996 Palm Pilot 1000 personal digital assistant

- 1996 Windows CE–based handheld device

- 2000 Ericsson R380 with Symbian OS

- 2002 Microsoft Pocket PC with Windows CE

- 2002 BlackBerry's first smartphone

- 2007 Apple iPhone with iOS

- 2007 Open Handset Alliance (OHA) forms by 84 companies including Google, HTC, and Sony

- 2008 OHA releases Android 1.0

- 2009 Samsung announces the Bada OS

- 2010 Windows Phone

- 2014 Microsoft releases Windows Phone 8.1

- 2014 Apple releases iOS 8

- 2014 BlackBerry releases BlackBerry 10.3

- 2014 Google releases Android 5.0 (Lollipop)

Pros and Cons

Native mobile application development on any platform has pros and cons.
The advantages are as follows:

- Better performance

- Easier development

- Easy money-making through built-in app store sales

Here are the disadvantages:

- Increased development time and costs

- Content restrictions and guidelines, based on the ecosystem

What Does the Market Say?

For the second quarter of 2015, the International Data Corporation (IDC) indicated the following share of the smartphone market (see www.idc.com/prodserv/smartphone-os-market-share.jsp):

- Android by Google: 82.8%

- iOS by Apple: 13.9%

- Windows Phone by Microsoft: 2.6%

- BlackBerry by RIM: 0.3%

- Others: 0.4%

Although these market details are based on the number of devices sold, application development still remains a problem. How are applications developed for all popular platforms today? As we discussed in Chapter 1, native application development is being overshadowed by hybrid application development. Figure 2-1 shows the basic differences between native and hybrid applications:

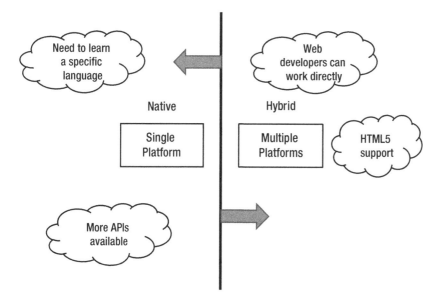

Figure 2-1. *Basic differences between native and hybrid applications*

Hybrid Mobile Application Development

In *hybrid mobile application development* (HMAD), mobile applications are developed using a technology stack and are packaged to deploy on many mobile devices with different screen sizes and manufacturers. Hybrid applications allow an application developer to build an application by using simple technologies such as HTML, CSS, and JavaScript. Sometimes developers use C# and VB.NET.

Hybrid mobile applications try to mix the best of both approaches; they use the power of server-side computing but don't treat the device only as a front end. These applications have a native component that resides on the device and can use the local features as if it's a native application. That is why hybrid applications are becoming more popular than other approaches.

Why HMAD?

Being able to develop once and deeply is often a motivation for using HMAD. Although we've discussed using the same code base, which seems easy, you still might need to change about 20 percent of the code, based on the platform. Why? Let's assume you are targeting Android and iOS at the same time. Sometimes the APIs used for the accelerometer, for instance, differ with respect to the platform. Some devices may not have the capability or sensor itself. Acceptance guidelines from Apple, Google, and Microsoft stores are different. Finally, UI consistency can still allow for differences on different platforms. Yet even this 20 percent of the code effort is much better than creating 100 percent of the code again. Because of this code reusability, HMAD is always better.

History

In 2008, Lee Barney, vice president of BDI, published a blog at https://tetontech.wordpress.com/ about communication between Objective C and JavaScript. Barney published code on the blog under the name UIWebView. In 2009, the iPhone 2 was launched along with WebView and SQLite database support.

In the same year, Nitobi (later acquired by Adobe) developed PhoneGap. PhoneGap became popular because of its capability to target iOS and Android. After PhoneGap, many platforms arrived on the market, making hybrid application development easier. This progress was built around JavaScript.

Meanwhile, plug-in-based web applications were as popular as mobile application(s). Adobe Flash and Microsoft Silverlight are popular plug-in-based approaches for the Web. Novel and Microsoft partnered to produce an open source flavor of Silverlight named Moonlight, based on the Mono .NET framework. Later Attachmate (a parent company to Novel) made a partnership with Xamarin. Xamarin as a product supports hybrid application development using C# for Windows Phone, Android, and iPhone. Xamarin hybrid applications use the Mono runtime.

Microsoft also offered universal applications for Android and iOS-based device(s) along with Windows Phone on the .NET platform. The Community edition of Visual Studio (IDE) is available for free with all features.

In June 2015, Apple announced Delphi for hybrid applications during the Apple Worldwide Developers Conference (WWDC).

Technologies and Frameworks Used in HMAD

Although, HTML and JavaScript are frequently used for HMAD, the following frameworks are used to communicate with device-based sensors, SD cards, cameras, and so forth:

- *Ionic*: This open source framework focuses on creating good applications in terms of patterns and practices.

- *PhoneGAP*: More of a packaging tool from Adobe.

- *AppBuilder*: This is a product from Telerik.

- *Kendo UI*: Framework from Telerik with the advantage of lots of rich UI widgets.

- *Sencha Touch*: One of the best framework platforms because of its built-in 50 UI components.

- *Angular UI*: Mobile Angular UI, similar to Sencha Touch.

- *Intel XDK*: This framework from Intel comes with an end-to-end development studio.

Based on the features required, costs, deadlines, expertise availability, and learning curve, you will decide which framework to go with. Xamarin is a new one that's been added to the list. However, it is yet to attain the same fame as the others. Xamarin also comes with an IDE and cloud-based testing features including performance analysis.

Pros and Cons

Hybrid mobile application development has pros and cons.

Here are the advantages:

- Platform-independent development

- Easier development

- Cost-effective

The disadvantages include the following:

- Limited device-specific feature-related APIs compared to native development

Summary

This chapter presented two ways to create a mobile-based application. One is native and the other is hybrid. This chapter also covered the frameworks available for building hybrid mobile applications.

CHAPTER 3

■ ■ ■

Building Blocks of HMAD

Each mobile operating system has a considerably different architecture of its own. Each app running in an OS needs to communicate with device elements, such as the sensors and cameras. When you develop native applications targeting a specific OS or ecosystem, you have to understand how services are offered by that OS or ecosystem (in the form of APIs), to access device features like sensors and cameras.

However, when you develop hybrid applications, the first step is to choose the hybrid application framework and then understand how services are offered by the framework, in the form of APIs, to access device features like sensors. Hybrid application frameworks can communicate with device components. Since most hybrid application frameworks are based on the concept of browser-based sandbox applications, you need to understand how the browser engine works and its limitations.

This chapter presents the basics required for hybrid application development.

Architecture

Because you're going to target mobile application development for three ecosystems—Android, Apple, and Microsoft—you first need to understand the building blocks of those operating systems. Then you'll look at how hybrid applications can be ported on top of each OS. In this section, you'll explore the differences between OS and browser runtimes.

OS Runtime

Each OS has a core component called a *kernel*. How is an API stack built on top of the kernel?
Let's explore this for the three main ecosystems.

Android OS Layers

The Android OS was built by Google, based on the Linux kernel. Figure 3-1 depicts layers in the Android architecture with a Linux kernel at the base.

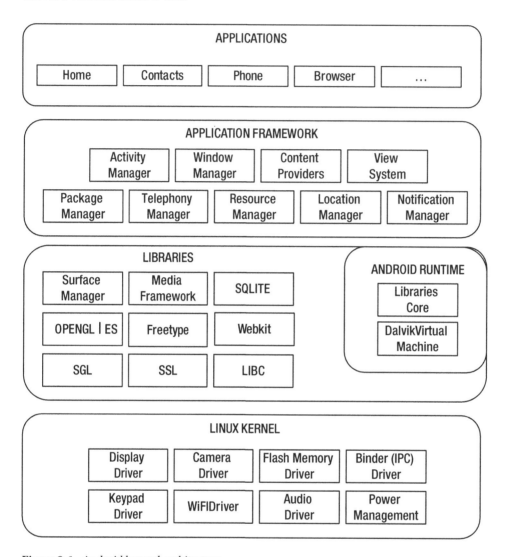

Figure 3-1. *Android layered architecture*

Any application built for Android natively will have to talk through an application framework layer. The code is run by the Android runtime and fed to it by a *Dalvika virtual machine*.

While coding for native Android applications, you have to use libraries offered by the SDK itself. WebKit and SQLite are popular examples. If you are familiar with the process of how Java works, it's mostly the same. A little extension to this understanding is required. Here are the details

Java

In a normal scenario, the developer has to code the application in Java. After compilation, the code gets converted into intermediate code called *bytecode*, instead of native code. Because of this, Java code can run on any platform; the code is not in native format, so it is yet to be converted into a CPU-specific format. After compilation, output is packaged and delivered as a JAR file. This is the end of development. When the JAR is delivered to the client, the code can't run directly, as it is not in native format. A machine on which it runs needs installation of a Java Virtual Machine, which in turn offers a just-in-time interpreter. This can convert the code from bytecode form to native form. The JVM is platform dependent, which makes the Java platform independent. Figure 3-2 shows the Java execution procedure.

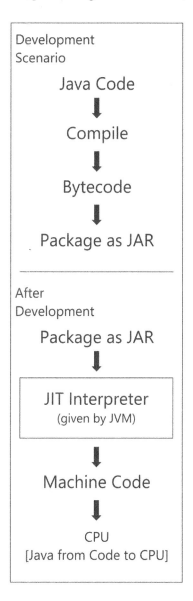

Figure 3-2. *Java execution*

Now that you understand how to make Java code work on different platforms, here is how Android uses a Dalvik Virtual Machine to run bytecode.

Dalvik

Android applications are preferred to be coded in Java, due to the Dalvik Virtual Machine. The bytecode after compilation is translated for optimized performance and stored in the file format DEX/ODEX, also known as a Dalvik executable. Published under the Apache license, the Dalvik runtime was used by Google prior to the KitKat version of Android. Google included a new alternative runtime called Android Runtime (ART), in the KitKat version. ART replaced the Dalvik runtime entirely in the Lollipop version of Android. Figure 3-3 shows the Dalvik runtime.

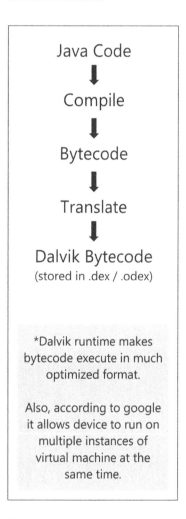

Figure 3-3. *Dalvik runtime*

So, this summarizes Android. Now let's talk about iOS.

iOS Layers

Figure 3-4 depicts the layers in iOS.

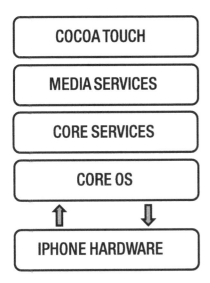

Figure 3-4. *iOS layers*

Each layer in this block diagram has features available, and to access or use those features, many frameworks are also available. Code written in Objective C or Swift does not directly talk with the underlying hardware. It has to talk through layers of the core OS in order get access to hardware. It is always recommended that you code at higher-level frameworks or libraries because there's less complexity involved while dealing with the hardware.

Cocoa Touch Layer

The first layer is the Cocoa Touch layer. This helps you to define the appearance of the application while porting on the iOSplatform. Various sets of libraries (frameworks) available at this layer help the developer handle different gestures and do multitasking.

Here is a list of features in this layer:

- App extensions
- Handoff
- Document picker
- Air drop
- Text kit
- UI kit dynamics

- Multitasking

- Auto layout

- Storyboards

- UI state preservation

- Apple push notification service

- Local notifications

- Gesture recognizers

- Standard system view controllers

This is the first layer you should evaluate while creating iOS applications.
Some useful frameworks (set of libraries) available in this layer are as follows:

- Address Book UI framework

- Event Kit UI framework

- Game Kit framework

- iAd framework

- Map Kit framework

- Message UI framework

- Notification Center framework

- Push Kit framework

- Twitter framework

Media Services Layer

This layer helps you use audio, video, and graphics in the application to implement a multimedia experience. Here is list of features in this layer:

- Audio

- Video

- Graphics

- Streaming

Some useful frameworks (set of libraries) available in this layer are as follows:

- Assets Library framework

- AV Foundation framework

- AVKit framework

- Core Audio framework

- CoreAudioKit framework

- Core Graphics framework

- Core Image Framework
- Core Text framework
- Core Video framework
- Game Controller framework
- GLKit framework
- Image I/O framework
- Media Accessibility framework
- Media Player framework
- Metal framework
- OpenAL framework
- OpenGL ES framework
- Photos framework
- Photos UI framework
- Quartz Core framework
- SceneKit framework
- SpriteKit framework

Core Services Layer

This layer helps you leverage cloud services, social media, and networking.
Here is a list of features in this layer:

- Peer-to-peer services
- iCloud storage
- Block objects
- Data protection
- File-sharing support
- Grand central dispatch
- In-app purchase
- Contents
- SQLite
- XML support
- Audio
- Video
- Graphics
- Streaming

Some useful frameworks (set of libraries) available in this layer are as follows:

- Accounts framework
- Address Book framework
- Ad Support framework
- CFNetwork framework
- CloudKit framework
- Core Data framework
- Core Foundation framework
- Core Location framework
- Core Media framework
- Core Motion framework
- Core Telephony framework
- EventKit framework
- Foundation framework
- HealthKit framework
- HomeKit framework
- JavaScript Core framework
- Mobile Core Services framework
- Multipeer Connectivity framework
- NewsstandKit framework
- PassKit framework
- Quick Look framework
- Safari Services framework
- Social framework
- StoreKit framework
- System Configuration framework
- WebKit framework

Core OS Layer

This layer contains the core APIs to help you deal with the underlying hardware. If you are using frameworks listed in these three layers, they are internally communicating with the underlying hardware through this Core OS layer. Very rarely do you need to use this layer.

Here is a list of features in this layer:

- Security
- Access to external hardware
- Acting as a bridge between other layers and hardware
- Some useful frameworks (set of libraries) available in this layer are as follows:
- Accelerate framework
- Core Bluetooth framework
- External Accessory framework
- Generic Security Services framework
- Local Authentication framework
- Network Extension framework
- Security framework

So, this was about iOS. Now let's talk about Windows Phone.

Windows Phone Layers

Windows Phone architecture has four main layers:

- Hardware at the base
- Windows NT kernel on top of it
- App - UI model
- Application framework at the top

Applications for Windows Phone are mainly developed in the Silverlight, XNA, HTML, and JavaScript frameworks. The majority of Windows Phone application development occurs with the Silverlight framework. XNA is used mainly for game development. HTML- and JavaScript-based native application development occurs less often than Silverlight.

To summarize, native mobile application development is through specific tools and languages, which always change with the platform. These applications always run closely with the operating system's runtime.

Browser-Based Applications and Browser Runtime

To understand the browser runtime from the perspective of hybrid applications, you have to understand browser-based applications. You use a browser for requesting pages from web sites and viewing the same. Every browser understands web pages, whether static or dynamic, as every page finally gets converted into HTML only.

The browser is a program that internally has a layered architecture, as shown in Figure 3-5. To provide a common understanding among all browsers available, the World Wide Web Consortium (W3C) defined specifications for HTML. However, many browsers only partially follow the standard.

Figure 3-5. Browser main layers

All browsers have key components such as the following:

- User interface

- Rendering component

- Browser engine

The user interface represents the browser's own look and feel, excluding the area where you can see the requested page. The rendering component involves an HTML parser, which, in turn, after parsing can generate the UI as well. The browser engine is the media between the user interface and the rendering engine.

Each browser, by default, understands HTML and CSS through the rendering engine. It also understands JavaScript code through a JavaScript interpreter.

The Problem with HTML

Older versions of HTML, before HTML5, have limitations in terms of what can be achieved. For example, playing a video using plain HTML tags or creating vector graphics was difficult.

Can we use desktop-based applications as they are in a web app? No and yes! No, we cannot, as the browser by default understands only an HTML UI, and desktop apps may not be HTML apps. Yes, we can use such applications, but plug-ins are needed to run them.

Due to such limitations, we never saw a new trend of browser-based applications such as Flash or Silverlight.

Flash

Adobe launched Flash (formerly called Macromedia Flash and Shockwave Flash) many moons ago, to create vector graphics, animation, browser games, rich internet applications, desktop applications, mobile applications, and mobile games. Flash would have survived only as a UI tool. However, understanding the needs of enterprises, Adobe also introduced Flex, which was equivalent to JSP/PHP, along with additional graphics-related functionality from Flash.

Silverlight

Microsoft launched Silverlight in 2007. It was equivalent to Flash, but offered more choices for coding. Since it was built on the .NET platform, every .NET web programmer could work in a language such as C# or VB.NET and create Silverlight applications. As for the UI, programmers had to learn XAML.

In Silverlight 3.0, Microsoft added a feature called Out of Browser. It allowed users to install the Silverlight application out of browser, on a desktop, with a single click. Users could find the application installed via a shortcut in the Programs menu. This feature bridged the gap between desktop and web-based applications, as Silverlight out-of-browser applications were safe and lightweight.

Microsoft also partnered with Novel to further extend Silverlight for open source, as Moonlight. Moonlight supported the out-of-browser application concept in the second version.

Flash and Silverlight—Good or Bad?

When these rich Internet applications got into the browser, they always worked in sandboxed mode, within the frame of the browser. Even when a Silverlight application is in out-of-browser mode, it always works in the browser's sandbox, but without showing the browser window.

However, it was possible to acquire additional permissions from the user to get exclusive access to the user's machine and file system. Whether it is Flash, Flex, or Silverlight, none of these types of applications would work on your machine (browser or mobile device) unless you installed the required plug-in or player to run it. For example, to run Flash on a user's machine, Flash player installation is required. To run Silverlight, a player is required.

Flash, Flex, and Silverlight were never in compliance with the HTML standard. Usability experts always complained about them.

Many browsers don't support installation of the plug-ins directly without user consent. This directly impacted the audience for these applications. The latest mobile devices contain more private data compared to desktops. Installing plug-ins can make users of such devices feel threatened. In addition, the Apple ecosystem bans the installation of plug-ins directly on the device. This means that a company developing web applications using Flash, Flex, or Silverlight loses a large set of the audience.

No one can say whether Flash and Silverlight were good or bad; they were a trend.

■ **Note** Although Flash required installation of plug-ins on the user's machine, almost 99 percent of Internet-enabled desktop machines have Flash installed (see `www.adobe.com/devnet/Flashplayer/enterprise_deployment.html`).

HTML5

Previous versions of HTML had limitations including cross-browser issues due to community-added tags and different ways of handling events by rendering engines. This was responsible for the trend of browser applications based on plug-ins.

Because some ecosystems ban plug-in installations, enterprises required another option. Hence we have HTML5.

HTML5 became a core markup technology standard for structuring and presenting content for the World Wide Web. The first draft of HTML5 was announced in 2009. The second and final draft was announced by W3C in 2014.

Figure 3-6 shows the evolution of this web standard.

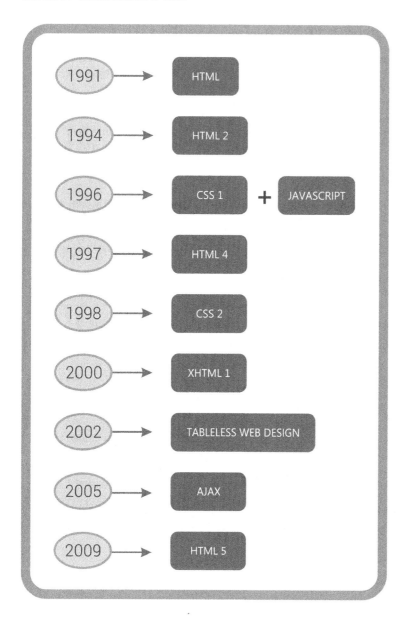

Figure 3-6. *Web standards evolution*

Enterprises gained the best of both trends: HTML and applications based on plug-ins for the Web. HTML5 offers the same by offering new tags and APIs in HTML. An API inside the HTML standard is a complete new offering! These APIs include location, offline storage, caching, and drag-and-drop.

Input controls became more powerful by offering built-in validation without using JavaScript.

The only problem with HTML5-based web applications is that they require browsers supporting HTML5. Figure 3-7 shows which API is supported on which browser.

HTML5 Embedded Content

Platform	Mac		Windows									
Browser	Firefox	Safari	Firefox				Safari	Chrome	IE			Opera
Version	3.5	4	3.5	2	3	3.6	4	2	6	7	8	10
Canvas	✓	✓	✓	✓	✓	✓	✓	✓	x	x	x	✓
Canvas Text	✓	✓	✓	x	x	✓	✓	✓	x	x	x	x
Audio	✓	✓	✓	x	x	✓	✓	x	x	x	x	x
Video	✓	✓	✓	x	x	✓	✓	x	x	x	x	x

HTML5 Web Applications

Platform	Mac		Windows									
Browser	Firefox	Safari	Firefox				Safari	Chrome	IE			Opera
Version	3.5	4	3.5	2	3	3.6	4	2	6	7	8	10
Local Storage	✓	✓	✓	x	x	✓	✓	x	x	x	✓	x
Session Storage	✓	✓	✓	✓	✓	✓	✓	x	x	x	✓	x
Post Message	✓	✓	✓	x	✓	✓	✓	✓	x	x	x	✓
Offline Applications	✓	✓	✓	x	x	✓	✓	✓	x	x	x	x
Query Selector	✓	✓	✓	x	x	✓	✓	✓	x	x	x	✓
Web Database	✓	✓	x	x	✓	✓	✓	x	x	x	x	x

Figure 3-7. HTML5-supporting browsers

Again, because of these limitations, development of applications supporting multiple browsers becomes difficult. As for HTML5-specific features, you may have to write JavaScript code to emulate the same features on a nonsupporting browser, or you might lose a potential customer!

Over the Web, problems related to HTML5 support won't exist if every browser vendor starts supporting equally, or end users upgrade their installed browsers to the latest versions supporting HTML 5. But since this is a new trend, why not leverage it?

HTML5 for All Development

Now that you understand that developing ecosystem-based mobile applications requires knowledge of a particular language and tool, web application development is trending toward HTML5.

Can you use HTML5 for installed mobile-based applications, as you can for web for desktop and mobile?

The answer is yes.

However, you have to consider certain obvious scenarios such as these:

- How will HTML5-based mobile applications be installed on mobile devices?

- Will these HTML5-based applications run under a browser context?

- What language will you use to communicate with the server or database?

- Will HTML5-based applications talk with underlying sensors?

- Will it be compatible with different screen sizes?

- And most important of all: Can HTML5-based applications target multiple ecosystems, as discussed previously?

To get an explanation for all of these, let's explore hybrid applications and how they work.

How Hybrid Applications Work

If applications for mobile devices can be created with the help of HTML5, what can be used for writing logic (for example, for connectivity to the server and database communication) is JavaScript. JavaScript, as per ECMA standards, has been around for many years.

Figure 3-8 depicts a hybrid mobile application.

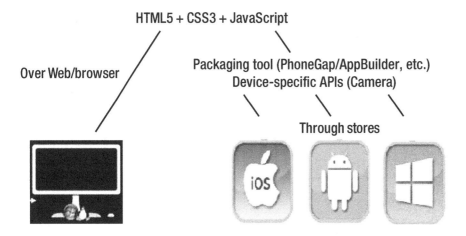

Figure 3-8. *A hybrid application*

An HTML5 JavaScript-based web application can be extended to access device-specific features and packaged using frameworks such as PhoneGap, AppBuilder, and Ionic. These frameworks also help to package the same app for different ecosystems, as discussed previously.

■ **Note**   Most hybrid application frameworks are based on top of the Apache Cordova engine.

If you want to write common business logic for web and mobile devices as well, authoring business logic as a service by using service-oriented architecture (SOA) is suggested.

Apache Cordova

Apache Cordova, from the Apache Software Foundation (ASF), is an API using JavaScript to access device-specific features such as cameras and memory cards. These APIs can be combined with frameworks such as jQuery and Dojo. Using this combo, you can develop applications for mobile devices without using languages like Java, Objective C, or C# (see Figure 3-9).

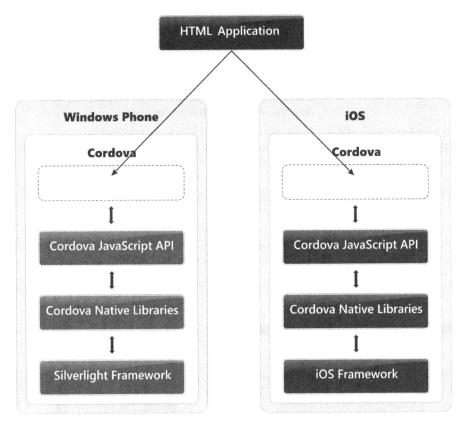

Figure 3-9. *How Cordova works*

Cordova provides JavaScript APIs, which in turn talk with Cordova's native libraries. It can be used in combination with UI frameworks like jQuery along with AppBuilder and Ionic.

The most important thing is that Cordova is open source. More details about Apache Cordova can be found at http://cordova.apache.org.

Web Applications vs. Hybrid Mobile Applications

Because HTML and JavaScript-based hybrid mobile applications use the same UI as that of their web versions, there are chances of confusion between both. Table 3-1 helps put the differences in black-and-white.

Table 3-1. *Web App vs. Hybrid Mobile App*

Web Applications with HTML/CSS/JavaScript	Hybrid Mobile Applications with HTML/CSS/JavaScript
Using these applications requires browsing the UI via the browser and raising an HTTP request over the Internet.	Using these applications requires first installing the application on the mobile device. Depending on the nature of the application, you may or may not have to raise the request over the Internet.
JavaScript code written with these applications cannot communicate with the client hardware, as it is restricted to run within the browser premises.	JavaScript code written with these applications can communicate with the devices and the client hardware, with permissions, by using an engine like Apache Cordova.
The user interface can be heavy.	The user interface has to be lightweight, as the UI has less real estate in terms of screen size.

Both can use the same UI, but that UI has to have responsive design (see Figure 3-10). Responsive web sites automatically scale the application's UI based on the device's screen size. You will see more details about the responsive UI in Chapter 7.

Figure 3-10. *Responsive web design*

Technologies, Frameworks, and Languages

Now let's focus on the technologies, frameworks, languages, data formats, and packaging frameworks used in building hybrid mobile applications.

HTML5

As we discussed earlier in this chapter, HTML5 is a new web markup language standard, announced in 2009 by W3C. The second and final draft, originally scheduled for 2022, was published early in 2014. End users are required to install the latest browsers on their machines with the capacity of rendering HTML5 tags and APIs. ·

The number of users upgrading to the latest browsers supporting HTML5 has dramatically increased since the first draft launch. Because the plug-in approach is about to become out-of-date, the future of HTML5 in the web world looks bright!

Why HTML 5?

Most browsers supporting HTML5 are almost consistent in showing HTML5 tags and APIs. Those browsers that are partially incompatible with this standard are being neglected by end users.

Many of the cross-browser issues due to vendor-specific tags (for example, <icon>) also will be automatically solved if the entire web world is driven by the same markup standard.

There is no need to write JavaScript code for basic validations, because of the new input types available in HTML5. HTML5 supports new input types such as email, color, date, time, and number, which do validation as well (see Figure 3-11).

Figure 3-11. *New input elements in HTML5*

For achieving functionalities such drag-and-drop and caching, you don't need to code now. More APIs are built-in with HTML5.

Basics of HTML5 and Useful APIs

As discussed, HTML5 has new markup tags. It also makes many old tags and tag attributes obsolete because of nonusage or alternative availability. Let's explore HTML5 basics and APIs.

To convey to the browser that the page is written with the HTML5 standard, the first tag is important. The line is as follows:

```
<!DOCTYPE html>
```

Following are the new structural tags in HTML5:

- section presents generic content in group format.

- article presents a self-contained composition.

- aside presents complete tangent contents (for example, advertisements) compared to the rest of the page.

- header represents a group of navigational aids.

- footer presents normal footer content.

The following are the new content tags in HTML5:

- figure presents flow content (which may be an image), with a caption preferred.

- video shows video data; supported formats differ, based on the browser.

- audio presents audio data; supported formats differ, based on the browser.

- embed is used for hosting an external application.

- canvas is used for rendering graphics.

The following are the new application-focused tags in HTML5:

- meter presents a range or scale of values.

- progress presents the amount of completion of a task.

- time presents a 24-hour clock.

- details is used for conveying additional information.

The following are deprecated in HTML5 due to replacement through CSS:

- big

- center

- font

- strike

- U

The following are deprecated due to accessibility:

- frame

- frameset

HTML5 Detection

You can detect whether HTML5 is supported on a client-side browser in multiple ways; for example, you can use TAG with inline content. If the tag gets rendered, HTML5 is supported. If the content gets rendered, HTML5 is not supported.

```
<canvas style="height:100px, width:100px, background-color=yellow">
       HTML 5 is not supported
<canvas>
```

Using HTML5 specific APIs, you can check whether the API works; if it doesn't work, you'll see the respective message:

```
if(typeof(WebWorker) == 'object')
{
alert ('HTML 5 supported')
}
```

```
else
{
alert ('HTML 5 is not supported')
}
```

You also can use the Modernizr library to check whether HTML5 is supported. Modernizr is a JavaScript library that can be downloaded from https://modernizr.com/. This library helps detect programmatically any HTML5 features available on the browser.

HTML5-Specific APIs

In HTML5, APIs can be divided into two categories: integrated and associated.

Integrated APIs

Integrated APIs may not require any script code. These can be directly used, and be presented through TAG or file. Such APIs include Video, Audio, and Drag and Drop.

Video

The video tag does not require a third-party plug-in installation such as Flash:

```
<video src="<VIDEOFILE.EXTENSION>" width="100px" height= "100px" ><.video>
```

In the preceding example, VIDEOFILE.EXTENSION represents the pattern used to provide the source. The following codec formats are recommended by vendors:

- H.264 by Microsoft and Apple (conversion through the HandBrake utility)

- OGG by Firefox and Opera (conversion through Firefogg on Firefox)

- VP8 by Google and Mozilla (conversion through the HandBrake utility)

Audio

The Audio API is used for playing audio content over the browser, without a plug-in requirement. Supported formats include MP3 and WAV. This API can help the user browse content offered from the server side offline. You can convey to the browser what kind of resources need to be in cache at the client side.

The file used for specifying the cache part is standard, and is named cache.manifest. This file is required to be provided with the HTML tag itself, as follows:

```
<html manifest="cache.manifest">
```

The cache.manifest file is shown in Figure 3-12.

```
CACHE MANIFEST
# this is a comment
CACHE:
index.htm
_css/main.css
_scripts/contacts.js
NETWORK:
updateContacts.cgi
```

Figure 3-12. *Cache manifest's sample cache file*

This can surely improve the performance of the application from the client's perspective.

Drag and Drop

This API enables you to drag one UI element and drop it at a particular container location. A few events (such as onDragEnter, onDragStart, and onDrop) need to be handled to achieve this action.

Associated APIs

Associated APIs require writing of the script code. Such APIs include Geolocation, 2D Canvas, Local Storage, Web Worker, and Web Sockets.

Geolocation

This API helps get the end user's current location. The API is added as an extension to the navigator object and provides methods such as getCurrentPosition() and watchPosition(). To obtain the position of the end user, permission is required.

The reply from the API consists of latitude and longitude, which later can be integrated with the Google Maps or Bing Maps APIs.

2D Canvas

The Canvas API can be used to draw 2D graphics. Geometry elements such as a circle, rectangle, and line can be drawn with the help of the Canvas API. Canvas becomes a base for graph APIs in many application frameworks including the Sencha Touch framework.

You have to use a 2D context to get the x and y axes before drawing. There is no 3D context available as of now.

Local Storage

In normal cases, browsers support cookies (small text files storing a user's profile data, such as login session ID or preferences). At a first visit, web servers and web sites may persist a cookie on the client machine to mark that the user has visited the server at that particular time. It may additionally store the user's preferences. Upon the site being requested again, the cookie information can be packaged by the browser and sent to the web server or web site, which then can be used to identify the client or user's preferences.

Although cookies are stored on the client's machine, they are always used by the server when sent back by the browser.

HTML5 offers a Local Storage API by extending the traditional window object. You can use this API to store about 5MB of data in the key/value pair format on the client's machine, based on the site's domain. This content can be accessed using client-side JavaScript. If the server requires it, the data has to be sent back through client-side JavaScript! So, this is a client-side API to store data.

Web Worker

Client-side JavaScript is always a single-threaded environment; multiple scripts can't run at the same time.

The Web Worker API in HTML5 brings threading to JavaScript. Now, you can run multiple scripts on the client side by using a web worker. You have to create a Web Worker object and assign a script to be executed as input in the form of a JS extension form.

Web Sockets

Over the Web, we use HTTP to communicate between a client browser and web server. HTTP is a stateless protocol; no continuous connection exists between the client and server. How will the server remember the client in the next trip? We use cookies and session concepts. Using these concepts, you can achieve stateful behavior.

The Web Socket API in HTML5 offers full, two-way (duplex) communication between the client and server. Underneath, it uses TCP. This becomes the base for web applications, which use video streaming or critical (or real-time), large data updates in the UI.

Data Formats

Whether you use HTML5 for web or hybrid mobile applications, communicating with the server is required for enterprise applications. If you consider hybrid mobile applications, then which format will you prefer to communicate with server? You have two industry standards available: XML and JSON.

Using XML

XML is a well-known standard defined by the W3C, way back in 1996. This standard became popular as many ecosystems launched APIs to support XML, including Microsoft, Apple, and Google.

After XML, browsers were launched along with an XML parser. Every browser supports an API for HTML as well as XML, called the Document Object Model (DOM), along with object support including Document, Window, and Navigator.

When JavaScript, as a client-side coding language, and DOM did not support XML natively, support was added externally by browser vendors including Microsoft, through the MSXML API.

Logic hosted on the web server and offered with the endpoints exposed is normally known as web services. Web services became the base for distributed enterprise applications. So, another thing that made XML more popular was web services.

Web services used XML over HTTP for communication, and were used as a middleware for cross-application platform communications such as Java and .NET.

XMLHttpRequest (XHR) was added in DOM version 2. Server-side support was built by many frameworks including Java server-side APIs and Microsoft .NET.

Drawbacks of XML

Though enterprises continue to use XML, it comes with one major drawback. Because XML data is always written in nodes, to those for whom only data matters, it seems to be carrying redundant parts.

Consider XML presenting an employee's data:

```
<?xml version="1.0" encoding="UTF-8"?>
<Employee>
        <Name> John </Name>
        <Id> 1928 </Id>
        <Age> 34 </Age>
        <Address>
                <City> Sydney </City>
                <Country> Australia </Country>
        </Address>
</Employee>
```

For someone who wants to know the data, knowing only that the John value stands for Name is sufficient. However, the XML syntax uses the end tag </Name>. Carrying this end tag as a set of characters makes the XML bulky. Using JSON format helps reduce the amount of data transfer.

Using JSON

JSON stands for *JavaScript Object Notation* The preceding XML about the employee can be presented in JSON as follows:

```
{ Name: 'John' , Id: '1928' , Age: 34 , Address: { City: 'Sydney' , Country: 'Australia' } }
```

As you can see, because you have no end tag as in XML, JSON format is shorter. Even complex data such as an address can be presented.

JSON format was formalized and made popular by Douglas Crockford. More details about the JSON data format can be seen at www.json.org.

Earlier there was no server-side support from popular frameworks like the Java server-side APIs and Microsoft .NET.

Over the Web, when a response is given by the web server, it always adds a content type. The default content type for response pages has always been text or html. As for XML, it was application or XML.

When JSON data used to arrive in client-side JavaScript, it was always taken as a string. Programmers used to get actual data by doing a string-split operation, until a helper file (json.js) was offered by Crockford.

DOM Version 2 Changes

Later native browser support was added for JSON in DOM version 2, along with an XHR object for XML. After DOM 2, JSON became a popular standard.

After the Android launch from Google, the smartphone market was shaken, with prices of the smartphone dramatically going down. Internet packs were made available by network providers at low rates. By then, smartphone users started browsing the Web over their mobile devices. Those web sites that used XML as a communication data format were noticeably slower than ones using JSON.

After this, using JSON in web applications became a trend.

Server-side support was added by many frameworks, including Java server-side APIs and Microsoft .NET. These APIs were used to convert framework-specific data formats into JSON, and also to understand the JSON passed from the client side.

Who Uses JSON?

Today web giants including Twitter, Microsoft, Facebook, and Google use JSON format for communication from server to client, and vice versa.

Reincarnation of JavaScript

Even mobile device versions of many web applications rely on JSON, because of the quickness and small amount of data transfer. Common issues with browsers include locating elements with specific classes, applying styles to multiple elements, and handling events in a cross-browser manner.

The tasks are possible in JavaScript but not easy to implement. Certain obstacles are guaranteed, including lack of expertise in JavaScript and lack of standard debugging practices.

The answer to all the problems discussed is jQuery!

jQuery

jQuery is a library based on JavaScript. It is written using JavaScript itself. Its code helps solve a major problem for a client script developer (the cross-browser issue).

jQuery library code can be downloaded from www.jquery.com. The jQuery library comes in two flavors: a development version and a production version.

You can even download the library from Microsoft or the Google Content Delivery Network (CDN) by using these URLs:

```
<script src="http://ajax.aspnetcdn.com/ajax/jquery/jquery-1.9.0.js"></script>
```

```
<script src=" https://ajax.googleapis.com/ajax/libs/jquery/jquery-1.9.0.js"></script>
```

jQuery provides several APIs to manipulate the DOM and handle events in a cross-browser way. It also heavily supports the JSON format. jQuery AJAX is comparatively easier than normal AJAX, with plain JavaScript.

jQuery Basics

Because jQuery is ultimately a library in JavaScript itself, If the client browser has restricted execution of JavaScript on the machine, even jQuery is restricted.

Like JavaScript, a jQuery library needs to be included in the script tag.

If you have to ask jQuery to search for an input text box with an ID such as txtName, then if you write the code as follows, the code simply fails. To use commands in jQuery, you have to use shorthand such as jquery or $. Of the two, use of $ is more commonly seen. Here, putting # before txtName means "find by ID."

```
--------------------------------------------------------------------------------
//....................HTML ............................
//....................HTML ............................
//....................HTML ............................

<script language="text/javascript">

var resultName = jquery('#txtName').value(),          //CODE FAILS HERE
alert(resultName),
</script>
//....................HTML ............................
//....................<txtName element> ......
//....................HTML ............................
--------------------------------------------------------------------------------
```

You would get an error conveying *undefined element 'txtName'! (Undefined what?)*

This means that jQuery tried to find an element with the ID txtName, but could not find one even if you had it in HTML!

The problem is that you're asking jQuery to execute the code way before the txtName control is loaded into the DOM hierarchy. So it cannot find it, because it tries before txtName is even created!

To ensure that the code gets called after the DOM tree and elements are loaded, you need to use the ready() function in jQuery as follows (replacing the preceding script block):

```
<script language="text/javascript">

        $(document).ready(SayHi),            //this will execute code in 'SayHi' function

        function SayHi()
        {
                var resultName = jquery('#txtName').value(),
                alert(resultName),
        }

</script>
```

jQuery prefers inline functions without names, which makes the jQuery syntax unique. The preceding script tag can be rewritten using jQuery's preference as follows:

```
<script language="text/javascript">
        $(document).ready(function ()                            //function without a name!
        {
                var resultName = jquery('#txtName').value(),
                    alert(resultName),
        }),
</script>
```

jQuery Selectors

One of the unique selling points for jQuery are *selectors*, which allow page elements to be selected. To find an element in HTML, you can use a different selector technique, as you used # in the preceding example, which denotes selection by ID.

Selector syntax is as follows:

```
$(selectorExpression) or JQuery(selectorExpression)
```

The following basic selectors exist in jQuery:

- To select nodes by tag name, use the tag name:

  $('div') selects all div elements

- To select nodes by ID, use #:

  $('#mydiv') selects elements with the ID attribute set to mydiv

- To select nodes by style class name, use .:

  $('.myStyle') selects all elements with CSS style class with the name myStyle applied

- To select nodes by attribute value, use square brackets:

  $('input[type="text"]') selects all input elements with type = "text"

- To select nodes by input nodes:

  $(':input') selects all input elements irrespective all their type

- Miscellaneous:

  $('table:tr') selects all <tr> elements inside the <table> tag

  $('tr:even') selects all <tr> elements that are even numbers

Table 3-2 shows some of the most frequently used APIs.

Table 3-2. *jQuery APIs*

Function Name	Description
.val()	Returns the content assigned to the value attribute of a tag; for example, input.
.attr('attribute', 'val')	Works as a getter/setter for a particular attribute of an HTML tag.
.css(json)	Sets the values of attributes of a style property. The bulk are set in JSON format.
.html()	Gets the inner HTML value of container tags, such as div.
.filter(selector expression)	Works as the next-level filter to get a specific element in HTML.
.toggle()	Toggles between multiple classes applied on the HTML element.
.append() , .prepend()	Appends or prepends the content to a container. The selector is a container.

While working with hybrid mobile applications, you'll be using a mobile-flavored plug-in on jQuery called *jQuery Mobile*. You will use more of jQuery in sessions to come!

Server-Side Support

Let's focus on server-side support while working on hybrid mobile device applications (see Figure 3-13).

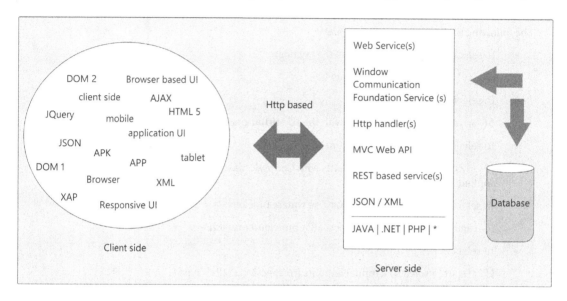

Figure 3-13. *Server-side support*

HTTP Handlers

This is one of the oldest techniques for consuming input data, executing business logic, and returning the respective data. In Microsoft .NET, this technique is called an HTTP Handler. This is similar to a PHP page without UI elements but with business logic. Also, it is similar to a Java servlet without a UI.

The drawback to this approach is that if many functionalities need to be clubbed into a single handler, the handler becomes a God class, which is not a recommended practice.

Service-Oriented Architecture

According to W3C, service-oriented architecture (SOA) is "a set of components that can be invoked, and whose interface descriptions can be published and discovered."

These components can be created and exposed with the help of frameworks such as Java server-side APIs, .NET, and PHP.

Web Services

Web services are web applications that do not produce HTML. They contain logic that accepts input in the form of XML over HTTP and reply in the same manner.

Based on who is going to call the logic or share the logic, and whether there are multiple clients, you can choose an SOA.

When you pick the web services approach, you first need to create a business component, which will be shared. This component can be called over HTTP. Data transfer happens strictly in XML.

This XML data transfer makes communication of web services with heterogeneous platforms like .NET and Java possible.

XML is transferred over an HTTP carrier. Technically, XML over HTTP along with a schema definition is referred to as SOAP (originally an acronym for Simple Object Access Protocol) .

Description of the service in the form of an XML document can be distributed so that clients can come to know about the methods or logic offered from the service itself.

Figure 3-14 shows the steps taken. The arrows in the figure convey whether the step is taken in the server or client context (or both).

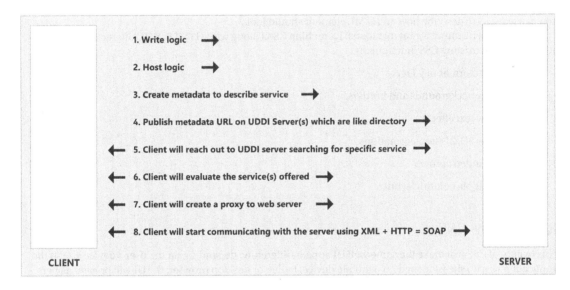

Figure 3-14. *Service-oriented architecture*

Even though it provided such a good service, the web services approach today is outdated.

When we have clients over the Web, putting logic as a web service serves the need. But when it comes to nonweb clients, web services lose out.

In 2006, Microsoft introduced another service-oriented approach, which is known as a unified communication platform or framework. The former code name for this was *Indigo*.

Windows Communication Foundation Service

Windows Communication Foundation (WCF) services have the following features:

- Service oriented, just like web services

- Multiple protocol support such as HTTP, TCP, .NET MSMQ, and P2P

- Multiple data formats are supported

- Built-in security APIs

- Reliable messaging using MSMQ (Message Queuing)

- DB transaction participation support

REST-Based Services

REST means *Representational State Transfer*. The main idea behind REST is that you should treat services as a resource. Also, you should be able to use HTTP to access those resources.

WCF with REST is an easy combination. REST offers end users the choice of XML or JSON.

Users can be exposed to all the CRUD (create, read, update, and delete) operations using WCF REST by decorating existing logic classes with attributes.

The REST-based format is also used by RSS/Atom feed reader tools.

Cascading Style Sheets (CSS) Version 3

You can use CSS to describe how an HTML element should look.

CSS has been around for many moons. Launching CSS3 along with HTML5, W3C offered the following additions to the existing CSS functionality:

- Selectors, as in jQuery
- New backgrounds and borders
- New text effects
- New 2D/3D transformations
- Rounded corners
- Multiple column layout

Responsive CSS

This feature of CSS will make the same web UI appear differently, depending on the user's device size. If the application or web site is opened on a mobile device, tablet, or desktop browser, the UI will present as per the real estate in terms of screen size available.

Twitter Bootstrap

Twitter Bootstrap provides responsive CSS along with a 12-column grid layout.

Instead of specifying the size of the control, you can assign the class name to the HTML element offered by Bootstrap CSS. These class names help the element occupy a length as per 12-column grid. The available screen size is normally divided into 12 columns. Based on the size requirement, each element is offered 1–12 column-level classes.

Skeleton

Skeleton is also a responsive CSS library with a 12-column grid layout available. The Skeleton library is simpler to use than Bootstrap. There are fewer UI tools available that work with Skeleton compared to Bootstrap.

HMAD Development and Packaging Frameworks

What is a packaging framework? While creating HTML5 and JavaScript-based hybrid mobile applications, you can choose the base and packaging from a platter of frameworks. Packaging frameworks help you create a final deployable output based on the ecosystem. The frameworks listed here also help port the same code on multiple ecosystems.

All these frameworks enable applications to compile on top of the Apache Cordova engine. Applications built on platforms are always going to run in web view.

This section describes some of the frameworks that are frequently used.

Ionic

This open source framework focuses on creating good applications in terms of patterns and practices. Ionic uses the AngularJS library for code purposes. It also recommends code in a Model-View-View Model (MVVM) design format, while presenting the browser (client) side alone.

Three layers exist in the MVVM design pattern, as shown in Figure 3-15:

- *Model*: JSON or XML data objects that may be received from the server

- View: HTML UI or CSS

- *View Model*: JavaScript code that can bind JSON or XML data (the model) with the UI (the view)

Figure 3-15. *How MVC layers talk with each other*

Applications created with Ionic include the following:

- *ChefSteps*: Cooking application

- *Mallzee*: Personal styling application

- *Sworkit*: Body and fitness application

More information about Ionic can be found at `http://ionicframework.com/`.

PhoneGap

Compared to any other framework listed here, PhoneGap is more of packaging framework. You can choose a JavaScript library for code like jQuery, plain JS, and AngularJS. After coding is done, PhoneGap can package the same, based on the need. PhoneGap is owned by Adobe and is based on top of the Apache Cordova engine discussed earlier in this chapter.

PhoneGap supports compilation in the cloud (using Software as a Service) without installing the SDK required for packaging applications based on ecosystems.

Some of the applications created with PhoneGap are as follows:

- *snowbuddy*: More of personal assistant or buddy type application

- *indoona*: Chatting application

- *jigsaw*: A jigsaw game application

More information about PhoneGap can be found at `http://phonegap.com/`.

AppBuilder

This product from Telerik was formerly called Icenium. AppBuilder has many similarities with PhoneGap, including having Apache Cordova at its base.

AppBuilder extends compilation-in-the-cloud functionality (just like PhoneGap) to offer code with tools such as these:

- Command-line interface (CLI)

- In-browser client

- Windows-based desktop application

It also offers a plug-in to popular IDEs such as Visual Studio and Sublime Text.
The following are some of the applications created with AppBuilder:

- *Survey Data Plus Plus*: Survey automation software

- *Birthplace*: Healthcare application

More information about AppBuilder can be found at `www.telerik.com/appbuilder`.

Kendo UI

Kendo UI is another professional framework from Telerik, but with the advantage of lots of rich UI widgets. Kendo UI has more than 70 UI widgets and more than a dozen built-in UI themes. It supports AngularJS and Bootstrap.
Some of the applications created with Kendo UI are as follows:

- *Udemy*: Education-related application

- *LunchBoat*: Social meal planning application

More information about Kendo UI can be found at: `www.telerik.com/kendo-ui/`.

Angular UI

Mobile Angular UI is just like Sencha Touch. An important fact to note is that it has tailor-made Bootstrap. Bootstrap does not directly offer sidebars or bottom navigation bars. Mobile Angular UI helps you get all of that along with Bootstrap! Mobile Angular UI is free and open source.
More information about Mobile Angular UI can be found at `http://mobileangularui.com/`.

Sencha Touch

One of the best framework platforms for building hybrid applications is Sencha Touch. Sencha Touch is a paid framework, which comes with more than 50 UI components often required in enterprise applications.

Sencha is fast in execution. It uses a Model-View-Controller (MVC) design pattern, considering code at the browser/client side.

It recommends using Ext JS, a JavaScript library.

The following are applications created with Sencha Touch:

- *TravelMate*: Travel domain application

- *Xero*: Mobile-based accounting application

- *Tubetweet*: A chatting and tweeting application

More information about Sencha Touch can be found at `www.sencha.com/products/touch/`.

Intel XDK

The XDK framework from Intel comes with an end-to-end development studio for mobile application developers. It consists of almost everything required for hybrid development including IDE, debugger, emulators, and deployment helpers. Code is supported using HTML5 and JavaScript.

Some of the applications created with Intel XDK are as follows:

- *Home Remedies*: Helper-in-life kind of application

- *Press and Hard*: A puzzle game application

More information about Intel XDK can be found at `https://software.intel.com/en-us/intel-xdk/`.

Testing Mobile Applications

Hybrid mobile application testers and developers may test applications for functionality, usability, and consistency.

Testing with Browsers

If an application is created with HTML and JavaScript, that application can be tested for functionality on a browser. The Chrome, IE, and Firefox browsers provide developer tools to debug and simulate certain behaviors.

The key challenge in this type of application testing is that the market has many devices with different screen sizes, operating systems, and so forth. How can you test applications for different mobile device sizes?

The answer is shown in Figure 3-16.

Figure 3-16. *Responsive web design over the Internet*

A developer who is running the application can use `www.responsinator.com`, to test the UI by using simulation.

Although working with a browser while testing has its advantages, you can't test device features such as an SD card or camera, because these features will be available only on mobile devices.

Hybrid applications can access device features when run in a *web view*; this means that though these applications are running in a browser context, they will always be running with elevated permissions.

So, you need to install applications on devices in order to test them.

Testing on Devices

If you need to test hybrid applications on iOS, Windows, or Android devices, each platform vendor will have different rules. Apple and Microsoft demand that you register for an Apple or Microsoft developer account.

Chapter 1 provides details on registration. Android may allow you direct installation by circulating the output file.

Therefore, testing applications for multiple devices is costly.

Testing with Packaging Frameworks

While developing application IDEs such as Visual Studio, Intel XDK may help developers and testers to debug or test applications. For an AppBuilder-like framework, you may get an extension to an IDE like Visual Studio.

These IDEs also come with emulators that help test the program on the dev machine itself.

After the testing phase is over, deployment of the application is planned.

Deploying Applications

Distributing an application in the Android ecosystem can be done freely and easily. If you want the app to be uploaded on Google Play, you must have a developer account.

When it comes to Apple and Microsoft, you are required to have a developer license. This allows one developer to test a specified number of applications on a single device.

If the application hosted is a paid one, then Apple, Microsoft, or Google takes a share in the minimum amount of money that you earn. Typically, the share ratio is 70:30.

Considering Cost

If your client wants an application to be put on iOS, Windows Phone, and Android devices, this native app development will be expensive in terms of money and effort because of the various compliance restrictions.

But when you decide to go hybrid, you have the following benefits:

- Less cost

- One code base

- Responsive code that helps build the UI for each type of device

- Less development time

Summary

This chapter covered the building blocks of hybrid mobile application development (HMAD). In the next chapter, you will create your first hybrid application by using Telerik AppBuilder.

CHAPTER 4

■ ■ ■

Creating Your First Hybrid Application

Objectives of this chapter:

- Understand packaging platforms for hybrid applications
- Understand server-side code writing
- How to use basic responsive CSS
- How to set up and use an AppBuilder account
- How to do local device testing

By the time you complete this chapter, you will have your first hybrid application working on Android, iOS, and Windows Phone!

Choosing a Packaging Platform

It's time to say hi by using a hybrid application. To create your first application, you need to set up a framework along with the packaging platform. As discussed in Chapter 3, many popular frameworks and tools are available for coding and packaging. Each has its pros and cons. However, because of its ease in coding and packaging, I prefer to go with Telerik AppBuilder.

Setting Up an AppBuilder Account

To get going, let's set up a 30-day trial account with Telerik. Here are the steps to create a trial account:

1. Visit www.telerik.com/appbuilder.
2. Click Start Now, as shown in Figure 4-1.

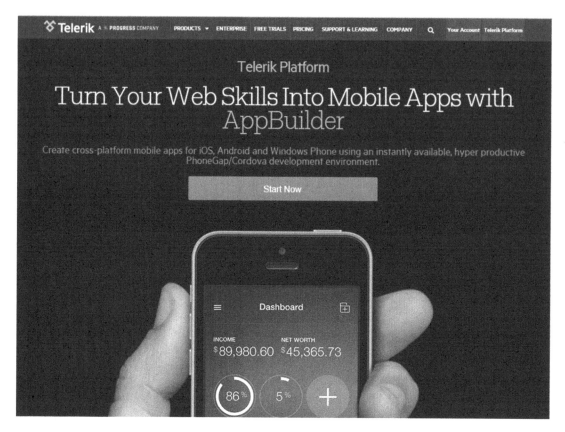

Figure 4-1. *First step: visit the Telerik web site*

3. Complete the registration form with the required details. I filled up mine as shown in Figure 4-2. Click the Launch Telerik Platform button.

Create an account

First name

mahesh

Last name

panhale

Company

bonaventure systems

Email

hybridapp@bonaventuresystems.com

Create password (5-1_ characters)

••••••••   ⊘

Launch Telerik Platform

or

Sign up with an existing account

✕̇ Telerik

8⁺ Google

f Facebook

⊞ LiveID

Y! Yahoo

Figure 4-2. Second step: new user registration

4. You might have to validate an e-mail account by clicking the URL that Telerik sends about an e-mail ID.

5. After validation, you may be navigated automatically to `www.telerik.com/account/`, as shown in Figure 4-3. (If not, navigate by yourself.)

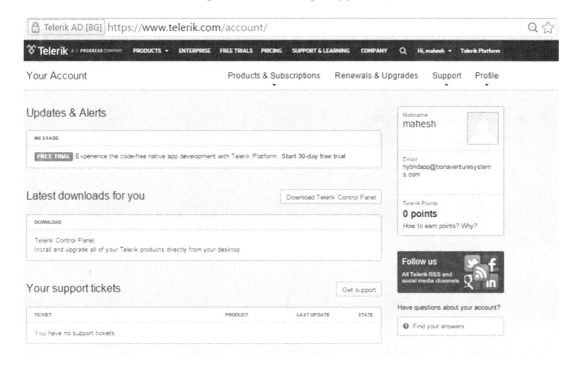

Figure 4-3. After e-mail verification

6. Click Start 30-Day Free Trial. If you want to purchase the product, visit www.telerik.com/purchase/platform. The price starts at $39 per month per user. The portal creates a workspace for the project and navigates you automatically to https://platform.telerik.com/#workspaces, as shown in Figure 4-4.

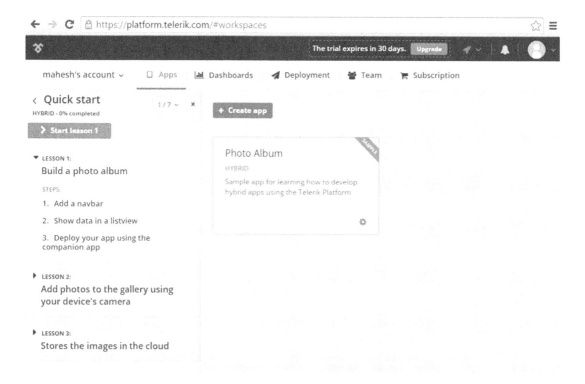

Figure 4-4. *Workspaces*

7. Click the Create App button.

8. The screen shown in Figure 4-5 appears. Enter details for App Name and Description as shown.

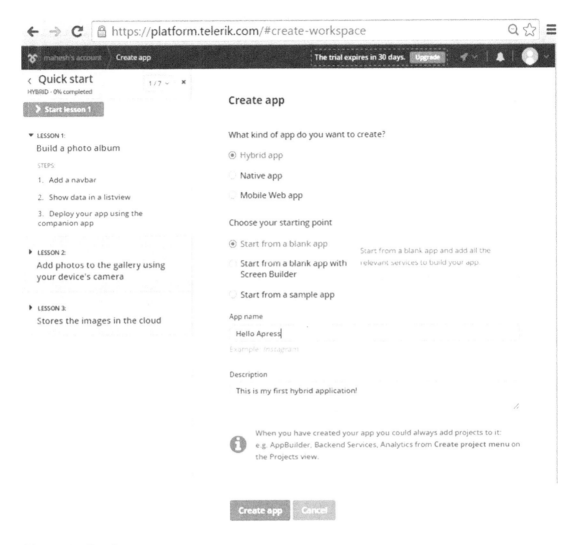

Figure 4-5. Creating an app

9. Click the Create App button. The next screen offers choices along with a short description about the project to be created.

10. Click the Create AppBuilder Hybrid Project button The next screen offers internal templates for hybrid projects. It includes Blank and a few with Kendo UI APIs added.

11. Choose Blank (the default) and assign a Name and Description for the project, as shown in Figure 4-6.

Figure 4-6. *Hybrid project templates from AppBuilder*

12. Click the Create Project button. After the project is created, the default helper modules are added into your project, and an in-browser solution window appears.

On the right side of the solution windows, you will find `index.html`. This is the file in which you will code the maximum number of times.

However, as discussed earlier, because you're going to call server-side code for getting data (JSON), you should first create the server-side code.

Let's revisit the client side of AppBuilder.

Authoring a Basic Service Returning JSON

We have discussed the importance of JSON over XML. You can return JSON format data by using either code based on service-oriented architecture (SOA) or by returning JSON as a content type from web applications built using Microsoft .NET PHP, ASP, and JSP. Let's start with the easiest way by creating an ASP.NET-based generic handler returning JSON data. If you are not from a Microsoft .NET background, you may use SOA base code to return JSON. (When used with Java server-side APIs, refer to `https://docs.oracle.com/javaee/7/tutorial/jsonp005.htm`.)

You are going to use Microsoft Visual Studio 2012 for the development. You can use an older edition such as 2010. The Microsoft Visual Studio Community 2015 edition is available for free and can be downloaded from `www.visualstudio.com/en-us/downloads/download-visual-studio-vs.aspx`.

An Express web edition of Visual Studio may also help.

Let's start by opening Visual Studio 2012 (Professional, Premium, Ultimate, or Express edition):

1. Create a folder named `\Apress\CH04\` on `System Drive` to store your project.

2. Choose Start ➤ Program Files ➤ Microsoft Visual Studio 2012. Click the Visual Studio 2012 icon. Alternatively, you can choose Windows ➤ Run and type the devenv command.

3. Click File ➤ New Project, as shown in Figure 4-7.

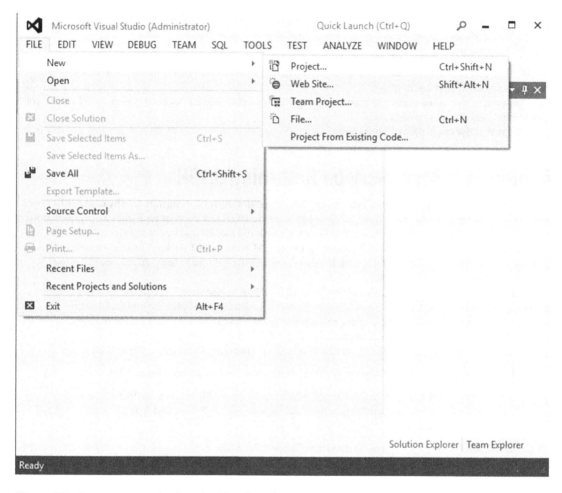

Figure 4-7. *Create a new project by using Visual Studio*

4. A New Project dialog box opens. Keep the default framework as is. From the left side of this dialog box, click Templates ➤ Visual C# ➤ Web.

5. From the right pane, choose the ASP.NET Empty Web Application project.

6. Name the project HelloServer.

7. Change the default location for the project storage to the previously defined folder. Deselect the Create Directory for Solution check box (because you've already have created one on C:\), as shown in Figure 4-8.

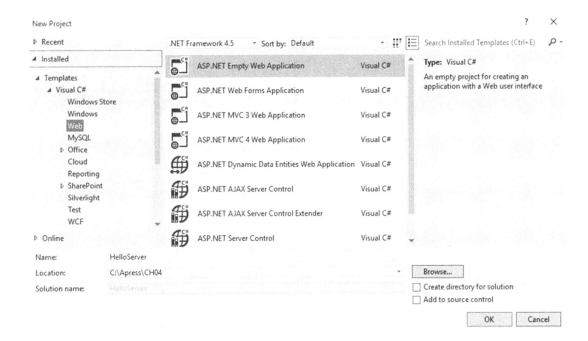

Figure 4-8. *ASP.NET empty project template*

8. Click OK. This action creates a project and opens a workspace like the one shown in Figure 4-9.

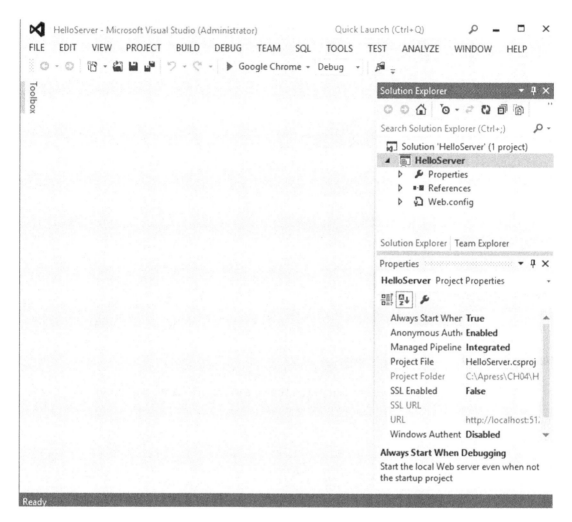

Figure 4-9. *HelloServer workspace*

9. In the Solution Explorer (at the top right of the project workspace), right-click the project HelloServer.

10. From the context menu, choose Add ➤ Class, as shown in Figure 4-10.

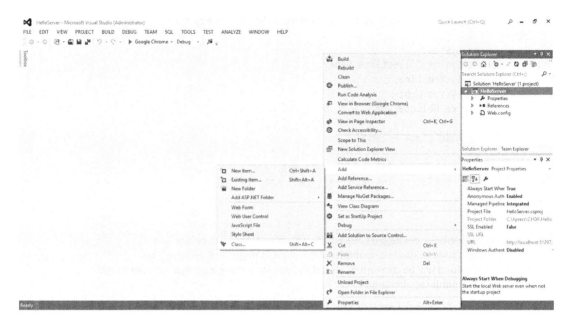

Figure 4-10. *Adding a class in the project*

11.   The Add New Item dialog box opens. Add a class file named `Person.cs`, as shown in Figure 4-11.

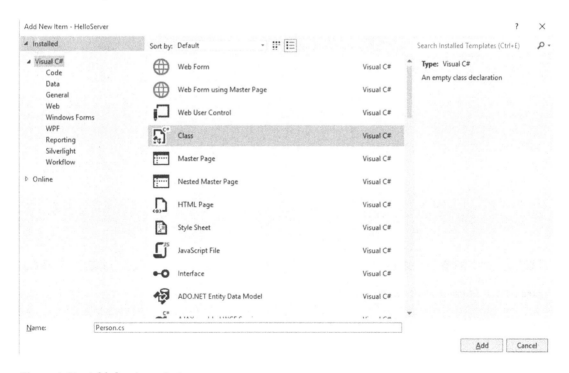

Figure 4-11. *Add class in project*

12. Open the Person.cs class file and insert the following code into it:

```
using System;
using System.Collections.Generic;
using System.Linq;
using System.Web;
namespace HelloServer
{
    public class Person
    {
        public string Name { get; set; }
        public string Address { get; set; }
    }
}
```

This code is for creating a class whose object will store one person's or one entity's (hard-coded) basic information, such as name and address. This information will be converted into JSON format by using a generic handler to our hybrid mobile application.

13. Again right-click the HelloServer project inside Solution Explorer.

14. From the context menu, choose Add ➤ New Item, as shown in Figure 4-12.

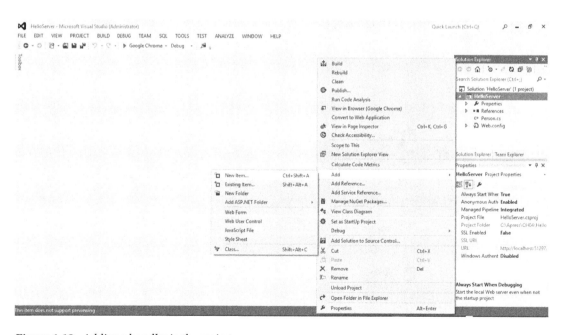

Figure 4-12. *Adding a handler in the project*

15. Select the Generic Handler template and name it `SayHello.ashx`, as shown in Figure 4-13.

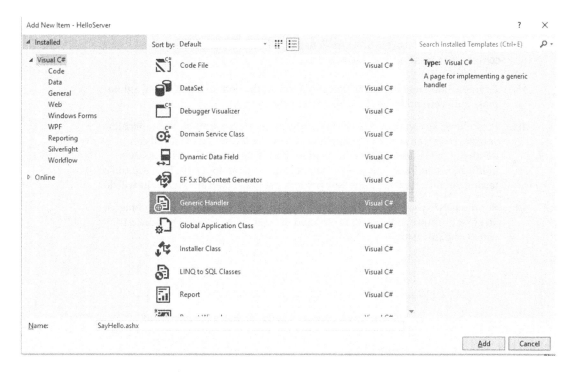

Figure 4-13. *Adding handler into project*

16. From the Solution Explorer, double-click `SayHello.ashx`. This opens the `SayHello.ashx.cs` file with the default code.

17. Remove the code inside the `ProcessRequest` method and replace it with the following code:

```
// Below line is to convey client browser / hybrid
// application that we are returning data in JSON format

context.Response.ContentType = "text/json";

// Create a person class object
// Assign dummy information to the same

Person person = new Person();
person.Name = "James";
person.Address = "London";
string jsonResult = string.Empty;

// Create Javascript serializer helper object
// Need to refer below namespace for the same
// Put using "System.Web.Script.Serialization"
```

```
JavaScriptSerializer jss = new JavaScriptSerializer();

// Serialize person's data in JSON format
jsonResult = jss.Serialize(person);

// Write JSON data to browser / App
context.Response.Write(jsonResult);
```

18. From the Build menu, choose Build Solution. At the bottom left of Visual Studio, make sure you can find a Build Succeeded message.

19. Press the F5 key on the keyboard to run the project. After you run the application, you can see a web server program, IIS Express, started automatically. It can be seen at the bottom right of the window, beside the taskbar and under the notification windows. This web server may run on a random port. Because you're testing this on a local machine, any random port picked up automatically will do.

20. Running IIS Express opens the default browser, which initially shows nothing, or an error, as shown in Figure 4-14. Append the URL in the browser's address bar with SayHello.ashx.

HTTP Error 403.14 - Forbidden

The Web server is configured to not list the contents of this directory.

Most likely causes:
- A default document is not configured for the requested URL, and directory browsing is not enabled on the server.

Things you can try:
- If you do not want to enable directory browsing, ensure that a default document is configured and that the file exists.
- Enable directory browsing.
    1. Go to the IIS Express install directory.
    2. Run **appcmd set config /section:system.webServer/directoryBrowse /enabled:true** to enable directory browsing at the server level.
    3. Run **appcmd set config ["SITE_NAME"] /section:system.webServer/directoryBrowse /enabled:true** to enable directory browsing at the site level.
- Verify that the configuration/system.webServer/directoryBrowse@enabled attribute is set to true in the site or application configuration file.

Figure 4-14. *Error: Forbidden*

21. Click Go or press Enter inside the browser. This action calls the server-side code and shows JSON code in the browser.

22. If you are using Internet Explorer (IE), it offers a download dialog box; to see the contents, you may have to download and open the same using Notepad. However, other browsers such as Chrome and Firefox may show JSON data directly on the browser itself, as shown in Figure 4-15.

Figure 4-15. *Viewing JSON in the Chrome browser*

23. Because you're testing the preceding code on a local machine, a random port will be picked up automatically and that will do what is needed. Run the application by pressing F5 on the keyboard. Visual Studio opens the default browser and displays the JSON, as shown in Figure 4-15.

24. Because this is server-side code and you will be testing and calling it on a mobile-based hybrid application using jQuery, local server hosting may not help. A local web server for testing purposes may not exist for all mobile devices. It does exist for Android devices. Refer to `https://github.com/jetty-project/i-jetty` for more information. Because of this limitation, you won't put it on a mobile based web server.

To help you call this server-side code returning JSON, you'll publish it on the live server. To do so, follow this Microsoft web site link, which will guide you in the publishing process: `https://msdn.microsoft.com/enus/library/dd465337(v=vs.110).aspx`.

To call this code, I published it on my company web site with this URL: `http://bonaventuresystems.com/Apress/BeginningHMAD/CH04/SayHello.ashx`. Figure 4-16 shows the output of the URL call on the browser.

{"Name":"James","Address":"London"}

Figure 4-16. *Viewing JSON in the Chrome browser*

Writing a Code Snippet Based on HTML5

Now, you have to write client-side (mobile-side) code. You will start by writing code for a plain HTML file on the local drive. This will help you debug and analyze the code.

If you attempt to write the code directly into the AppBuilder project workspace, debugging it would be difficult as it compiles into the cloud and lets you download the final output based on the targeted device chosen.

So, let's create a new folder named HelloClient under the earlier defined folder.

Follow these steps to complete the HTML5 code snippet:

1. Add a new text document, New Text Document.txt into the folder <SYSTEM DRIVE>:\Apress\CH04\ HelloClient.

2. Rename New Text Document.txt to index.html. Make sure you change the file extension!

3. To complete the resources required for the project, you'll download the jQuery library. You'll learn more about the jQuery library in the next section. Visit https://jquery.com/.

4. From the Download tab, download the latest version of this library (1.11.3 at the time of this writing). The library is free.

5. From http://getbootstrap.com/, download the CSS3-based Twitter library, bootstrap.css.

6. Extract the compressed file and keep only bootstrap.min.css and bootstrap. min.js in the HelloClient folder. You will learn more about Bootstrap CSS in next section. The structure and content of the HelloClient folder are shown in Figure 4-17.

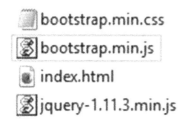

Figure 4-17. *HelloClient folder structure*

7. Start Visual Studio as you did previously. Click File ➤ Open ➤ File (or press Ctrl+O), as shown in Figure 4-18.

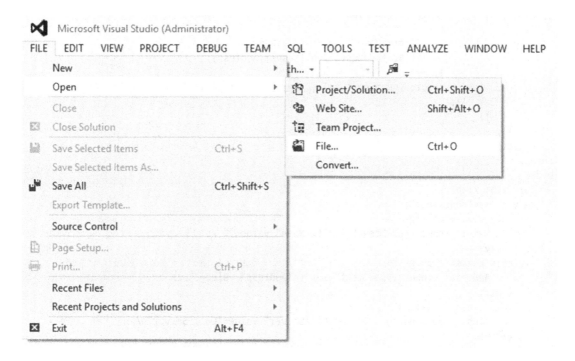

Figure 4-18. *Opening a file by using Visual Studio*

8. This action opens a dialog box. Browse to the HelloClient folder created earlier. Select index.html and then click the Open button.

9. Insert the following code into the index.html page:

```
<!DOCTYPE html>
<html>
<head>
    <title>Say Hi</title>
    <script src="jquery-1.11.3.min.js"></script>
    <link rel="stylesheet" href="bootstrap.min.css" />
    <script src="bootstrap.min.js"></script>
    <script>
        $(document).ready(function () {
            $('#btnCallServer').click(function () {
                $.ajax({
                    url: 'http://bonaventuresystems.com/Apress/BeginningHMAD/CH04/
                        SayHello.ashx',
                    type: 'GET',
                    success: function (result)
                    {
                        $('#txtName').val(result.Name);
                        $('#txtAddress').val(result.Address);
                    },
                    error: function (err) { alert('Error!'); }
                });
            });
        });
    </script>
</head>
<body>
    <br /><br /><br />
    <div class="container">
        <div class="col-lg-3">
            Name: <input type="text" id="txtName" value="" />
        </div>
        <div class="col-lg-3">
            Address: <input type="text" id="txtAddress" value="" />
        </div>
        <div class="col-lg-3">
            <input type="button" id="btnCallServer" value="Call Server" />
        </div>
    </div>
</body>
</html>
```

10. Right click anywhere inside the code window (inside Visual Studio) and then select the View in Browser option. The default browser opens and shows the rendered HTML5-based output, as shown in Figure 4-19.

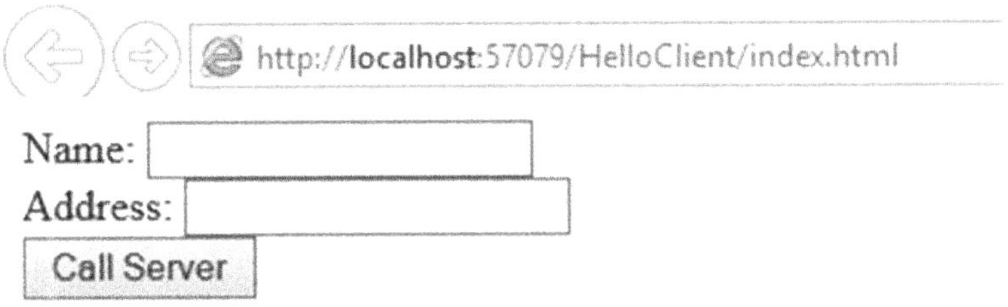

Figure 4-19. *Running index.html on localhost using Internet Explorer*

11. This is the browser-based UI for your application. A similar UI will be available on the mobile screen, but you won't see a browser window at all. Keep it in mind that the server still returns output in JSON data format. Now, when you click the Call Server button, the code throws an error. To get more details easily, let's use Google Chrome's developer tools. Open the Google Chrome browser.

12. Type the same URL that was there while you ran `index.html` using Visual Studio. The URL is similar to what you see in Figure 4-19. (The port number may be different on your machine.) The UI looks like Figure 4-20.

Figure 4-20. *Run index.html on localhost using Google Chrome*

13. Now, before clicking the Call Server button, let's open the developer tools. Either press F12 on the keyboard or click the Customize and Control Google Chrome button at the right corner of the address bar. Then click More Tools ➤ Developer Tools, as shown in Figure 4-21. After the developer tools are open, the Chrome browser will look like Figure 4-22.

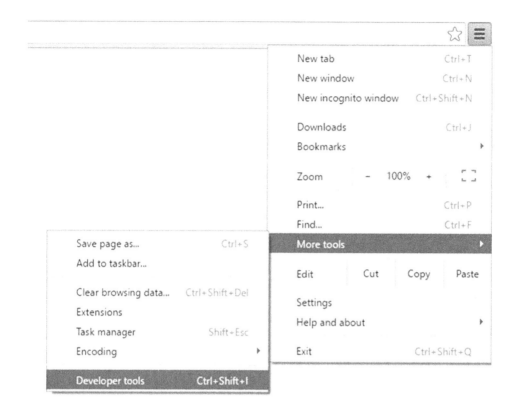

Figure 4-21. *Opening developer tools on Google Chrome*

Figure 4-22. *Google Chrome with developer tools*

14. Click the Call Server button. An error occurs as it did earlier in Internet Explorer, as shown in Figure 4-23.

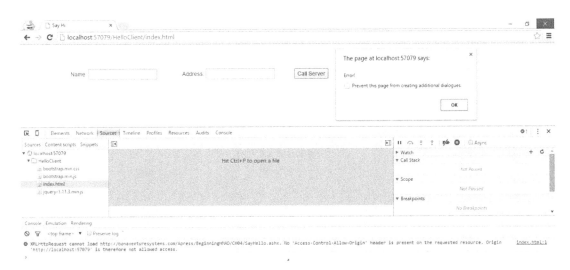

Figure 4-23. *Tracking the error on Google Chrome*

15. You can see the error details in the console window at the bottom, in default red characters. The error details convey the following:

```
XMLHttpRequest cannot load http://bonaventuresystems.com/Apress/
BeginningHMAD/CH04/SayHello.ashx. No 'Access-Control-Allow-Origin'
header is present on the requested resource. Origin 'http://
localhost:57079' is therefore not allowed access.
```

This means that the server-side code that is on the domain bonaventuresystems.com does not permit calls from another domain (in this case, localhost:57079). This is a common issue with cross-origin calls, or calls made from one domain to another domain. Such calls have to be permitted through code. So you need to allow calls to SayHello.ashx (bonaventuresystems) from the pages that belong to a different origin (localhost:57079).

16. How to do it? It's simple. The solution is given in the error message itself. You have to add one extra line of code at the very end of the ProcessRequest method of SayHello.ashx:

```
context.Response.AppendHeader("Access-Control-Allow-Origin", "*");
```

This line allows calls to `SayHello.ashx` as a resource from any other domain, as you have specified * in second parameter. After deploying the latest and revised `SayHello.ashx` file on BonaventureSystems.com, now when you click the Call Server button, the code ends in Success! After redeployment, the output looks like Figure 4-24.

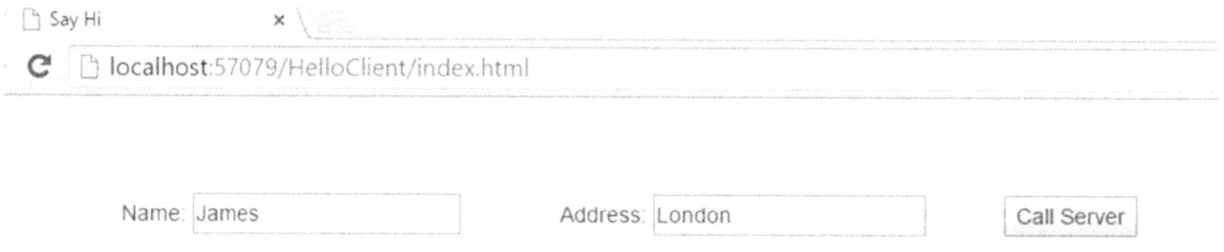

Figure 4-24. *After solving a cross-origin error*

Let's now explore the important lines of HTML, jQuery, and Bootstrap code injected in `index.html`. This line conveys to the browser that the HTML page is written adhering to the HTML5 standard:

```
"<!DOCTYPE html>"
"<script src="jquery-1.11.3.min.js"></script>
   <link rel="stylesheet" href="bootstrap.min.css" />
 <script src="bootstrap.min.js"></script>"
```

Here referencing sequence matters:

- `bootstrap.min.js` uses `bootstrap.min.css` and is dependent on the jQuery library. The code references the latest jQuery version, 1.11.3.

- `min` denotes that the respective file contents are minified (reduced in size) and that the file is a production-level file.

Injecting jQuery into the Code

$ is shorthand syntax for jQuery. The following line asks jQuery to execute a function (which does not have a name—it's anonymous). This function executes only after the Document Object Model tree (DOM tree) is ready. In simple words, it indicates to execute the function code when all controls in the HTML are loaded in the hierarchy.

```
"$(document).ready(function () {.........})"
```

The next line throws an error if it's not written after the preceding "document ready" line. This line asks jQuery to find a control in the HTML hierarchy with an ID attribute value of `btnCallServer`. The # before `btnCallServer` conveys finding by ID. Further, this line also conveys a function (again which does not have a name—it's anonymous), which needs to be called only when a Click event is raised with `btnCallServer`.

```
$('#btnCallServer').click(function () {
```

The next line makes an AJAX asynchronous call to bonaventuresystems.com/SayHello.ashx and collects the JSON data in an anonymous function conveyed after the success word.

$.ajax(....)

Also, the error is captured in a similar way. In short, the parameters convey the following:

- url: What to call?

- type: How to call (GET, POST, PUT, or DELETE)

- success: What to call after a successful reply from the server

- error: What to call after an error received from the server

In the following HTML, styles are added using classes given by bootstrap.css:.

```
<div class="container">
    <div class="col-lg-3">
        Name: <input type="text" id="txtName" value="" />
    </div>
    <div class="col-lg-3">
        Address: <input type="text" id="txtAddress" value="" />
    </div>
    <div class="col-lg-3">
     <input type="button" id="btnCallServer" value="Call
     Server" />
    </div>
</div>
```

These classes help you achieve a responsive UI! Although this code uses only a few classes out of many, the appearance of the UI and the alignment of the controls changes based on the screen of the device.

For example, when this application's UI is seen on mobile devices and tablets, the alignment of the controls is not a cause for concern because of the responsive UI.

To understand the importance of this library, let's look at how this page will look on different devices of different sizes! Let's do the early testing!

Testing the Hybrid Application UI and Code by Using a Browser

1. Copy the index.html URL: http://localhost:57079/HelloClient/index.html.

2. Open any browser to www.responsinator.com.

3. Type the index.html URL from step 1 in the Enter Your Site text box, as shown in Figure 4-25. Then click Go.

Figure 4-25. Enter the site URL in the responsinator

Notice how responsive the UI looks on different devices, as shown in Figure 4-26. The responsinator helps display the UI for many screens.

Figure 4-26. *Responsive web design in the responsinator*

So all that you've done has tested the code on the browser. But, remember, you are deploying a mobile application! Now, let's package the application using AppBuilder.

Packaging an Application for the First Time Using AppBuilder

Previously in this chapter, you created a trial account on the Telerik web site. Follow these steps to complete the demo packaging:

1. Open the index.html file inside the Apress Project folder.

2. Replace the code in index.html with the code that you wrote using Visual Studio, as shown in Figure 4-27.

Figure 4-27. *Code in index.html*

3. Inside Solution Explorer, right-click Apress Project and then select Add ➤ Existing Files, as shown in Figure 4-28. The dialog box shown in Figure 4-29 opens.

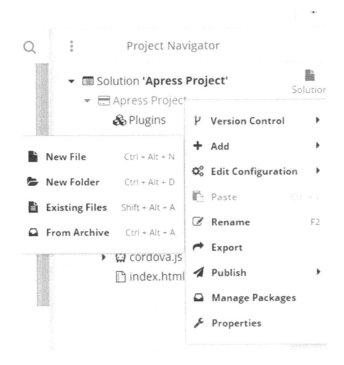

Figure 4-28. *Adding existing files*

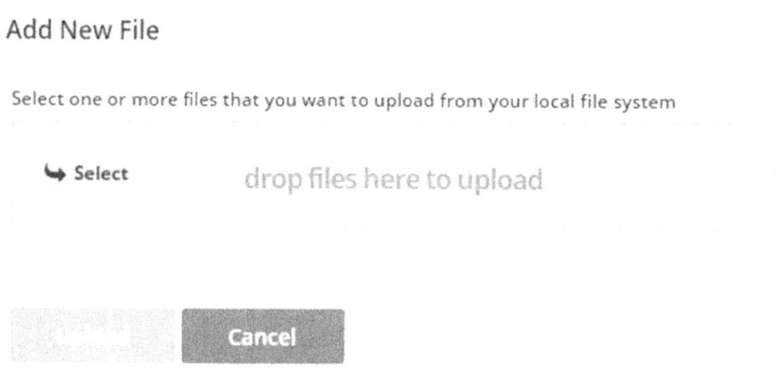

Add New File

Select one or more files that you want to upload from your local file system

↳ Select   drop files here to upload

Cancel

Figure 4-29. *Adding existing resourcess*

4. As shown in Figure 4-30, from the `HelloClient` folder, either drag and drop the following files, or click Select and then browse for and upload these three files:

   • `bootstrap.min.css`

   • `bootstrap.min.js`

   • `jquery-1.11.3.min.js`

Add New File

Select one or more files that you want to upload from your local file system

↳ Select   drop files here to upload

bootstrap.min.css

bootstrap.min.js

jquery-1.11.3.min.js

Upload   Cancel

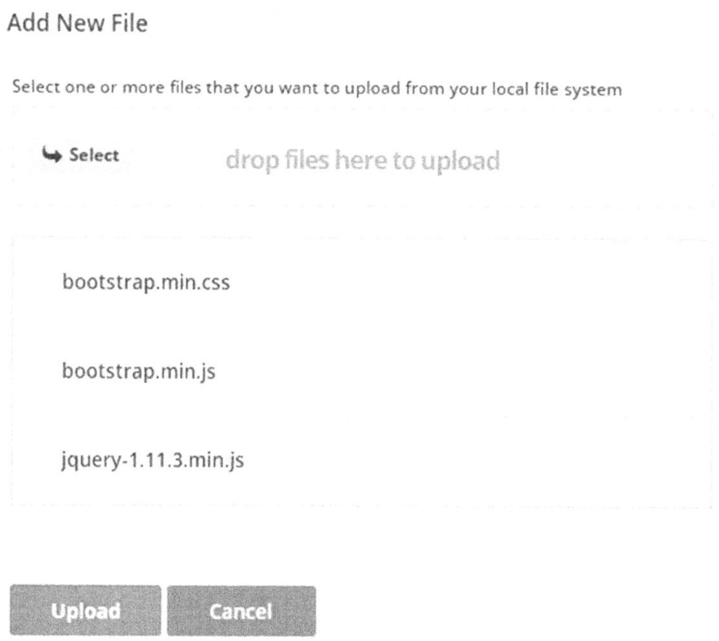

Figure 4-30. *Adding existing resourcess*

You don't have to add index.html, as you already copied its contents into the default index.html from Solution Explorer. Solution Explorer will look like Figure 4-31.

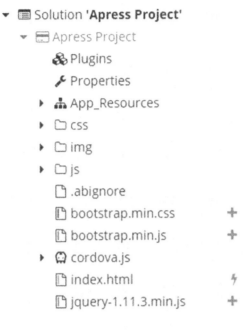

Figure 4-31. Solution after adding existing resources

5.   Click the Run button. You get the option to either Build or to test the application on various simulators. Let's test using an iPhone simulator, as shown in Figure 4-32.

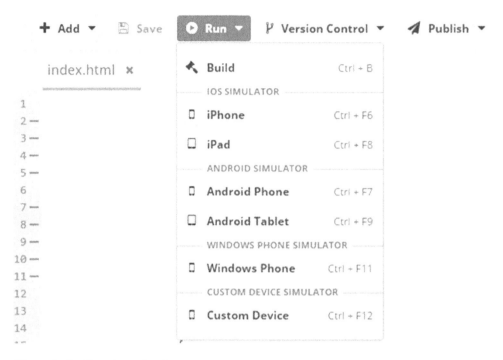

Figure 4-32. *Choosing a simulator*

6. This selection opens the iPhone simulator in a pop-up window, as shown in Figure 4-33. Click the Call Server button to see the result.

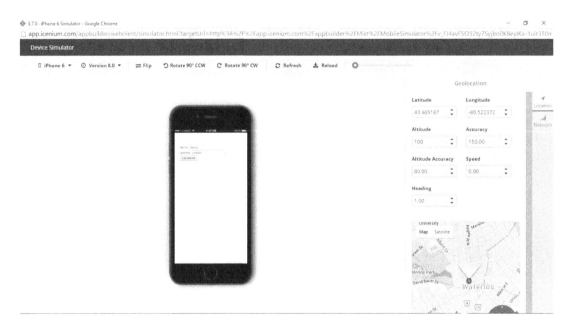

Figure 4-33. *iPhone simulator*

7. From the top-left panel in the pop-up window, change iPhone to Android Phone, as shown in Figure 4-34. Then test in a similar way, as shown in Figure 4-35.

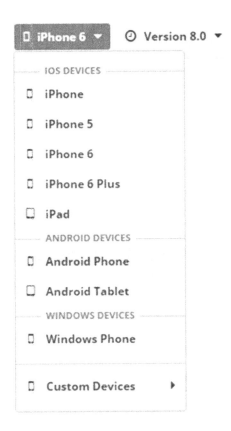

Figure 4-34. *Changing the simulator*

Figure 4-35. *Using the Android simulator*

8. Do the same for Windows Phone, as shown in Figure 4-36.

Figure 4-36. *Windows Phone simulator*

9.   Close the pop-up. Choose Run ➤ Build, as shown in Figure 4-37.

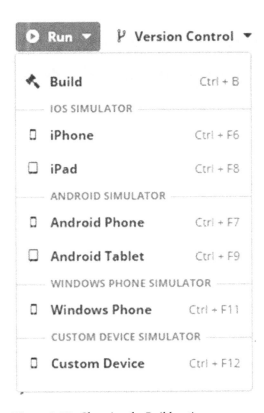

Figure 4-37. *Choosing the Build option*

10.   A pop-up opens, enabling you to choose a platform for packaging. For this example, choose Android, as shown in Figure 4-38.

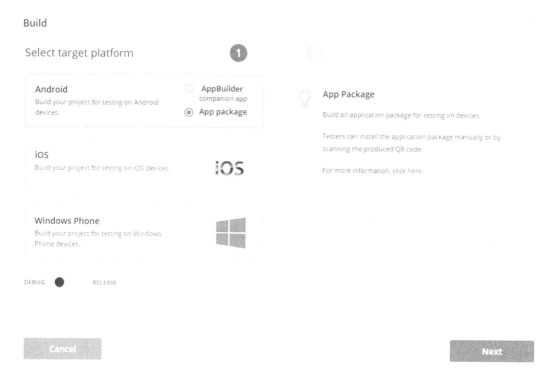

Figure 4-38. *Android packaging*

At this point, you need to understand the options. If you choose iOS or Windows Phone, packaging won't be as smooth as with Android. Why? iOS application packaging using AppBuilder requires that you code sign the application before it gets published!

The process for code signing is explained on the Telerik web site: `http://docs.telerik.com/platform/ appbuilder/code-signing-your-app/configuring-code-signing-for-ios-apps/configuring-code- signing-for-ios-apps`

Windows Phone application packaging using AppBuilder requires a Telerik application enrollment token.

The process for getting a Telerik application enrollment token is explained on the Telerik web site at the following link: `http://docs.telerik.com/platform/appbuilder/`.

11. When publishing for Android, you have two options for the final package, as you can see in the pop-up window:

   - *Using AppBuilder*: With this approach, you need to have the AppBuilder application installed on the client's hybrid mobile application package, or the installer will be pushed through the AppBuilder application.

   - *Using AppPackage*: This approach asks the client to download and install the final output file directly.

12. You need to indicate whether you're finished with the application or still in the development phase. Choose Debug or Release mode.

13. Click the Next button; this starts the build and packaging of the code in the cloud. You can see the progress, as shown in Figure 4-39. When the build is complete, the screen in Figure 4-40 displays.

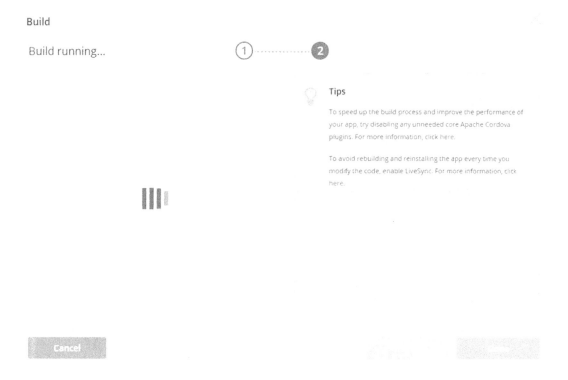

Figure 4-39. *Progress of the Android packaging*

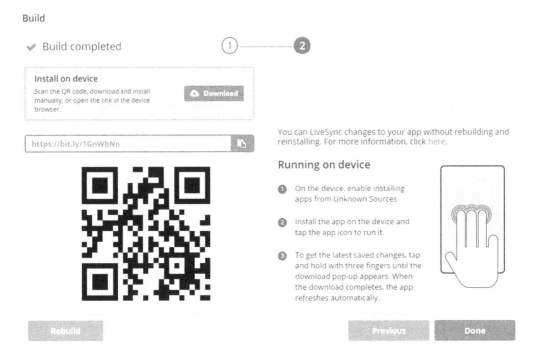

Figure 4-40. *Completed Android packaging*

14. Click the Download button, and the final output is shown on the machine, as you can see in Figure 4-41.

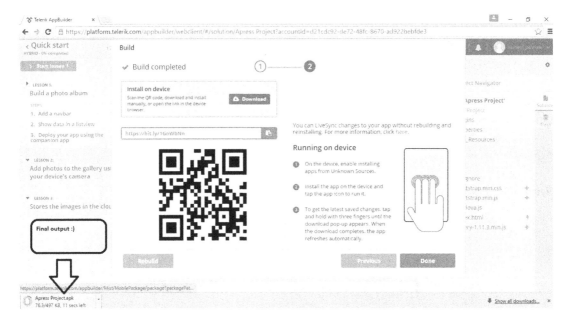

Figure 4-41. *Final packaging output*

Running a Local Test on the Device

After your package is ready, testing it on a real device requires meeting certain prerequisites of the platforms vendors. For example, the most common requirement is to purchase a developer license from the platform vendor. Costs vary from vendor to vendor. Let's explore these licensing terms, costs, and obstacles while working on the major platforms.

iPhone

To publish applications at the App Store, Apple offers a membership program. Membership is available to individuals, organizations, and educational institutions. Fees are always annual; for an individual, the developer program fee is $99 per year. The cost varies for organizations and educational institutions.

The Apple web site says, "This Membership includes access to beta OS releases, advanced app capabilities, and tools to develop, test, and distribute apps and Safari extensions. Developers enrolled as individuals will sell apps on the App Store using their personal name."

Normally, 100 installations for each device (iPhone, iPad, iPod, and Apple watch) for testing purposes are allowed for each developer license per membership year.

If the app is paid, Apple gets 30 percent of the cost, and the developer takes 70 percent.

More details are available at `https://developer.apple.com/programs/whats-included/`.

Android

To publish applications on Google Play (formerly the Google Play Store or Android Market), Google offers a membership program. The one-time fee for a publisher account is $25.

You can transfer app output files (APKs) directly to an Android mobile device by using an SD card, the Internet, or Bluetooth without this license. The licensé is required if you want to publish apps through Google Play.

The revenue model remains the same as that of Apple. More details are available at `http://developer .android.com/distribute/googleplay/start.html`.

Windows Phone

To publish applications on the Windows Store, Microsoft offers a membership program. An individual account costs $19 per year. A company account costs $99 per year.

More details are available at `https://msdn.microsoft.com/en-in/library/windows/apps/jj863494.aspx`.

Summary

Although many packaging platforms exist, in this chapter you created a simple application with the help of the AppBuilder platform from Telerik.

Using JavaScript in a flavored form such as jQuery, CSS3 in the form of responsive CSS like Twitter, along with HTML5-based UI markup has become a trend nowadays for hybrid mobile application development.

You'll learn about the internals of HMAD in the next chapter.

■ ■ ■

HMAD: Internals

The objectives of this chapter are to

- Learn about general communication layers in hybrid applications on mobile OS

- Learn how hybrid applications work

- Learn about webview obstacles

- Provide recommendations

This chapter covers many of the good and the bad aspects of hybrid applications. It begins with how hybrid mobile applications work and then teaches the concept of webviews on mobile.

Mobile Devices

So far, the focus of this book has been on Android, iPhone, and Windows Phone. However, hybrid applications can be deployed on LG webOS, Fire OS, Blackberry, and so forth. Android has been considered our main target platform because it is has more users than the iPhone and Windows Phone. However, Microsoft technologies will be the focus of most of the server-side code.

Architecture

We can generalize layered and native application architecture by considering layers. The top layer in Figure 5-1 denotes the application created using the device's preferred languages, for example, Java for Android.

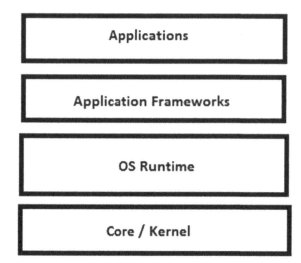

Figure 5-1. *General native application architecture*

The application framework can act as a mediator between OS, device features, and the application.

However, when it comes to hybrid applications, one very specific component plays an important role: the webview. We are going to see more about this component later in this chapter.

Based on the goal to provide native device features to the hybrid application, we may have different architectural approaches. We are going to discuss these approaches in this chapter.

Approach: Define a custom framework or plug-in—on top of WebKit or the Trident engine—that can be used further to access device features. This framework may use a channel or socket, through which messaging can take place, since the WebKit engine is not common to all. It works for Chrome and Safari, which means the Android and the iPhone. Analogically, this approach is more like plug-in development on a browser with permissions to access device features.

Approach: Use the webview control provided by the vendor. It can render the UI contents as well. Access to native device features is not directly available by using only a webview. External components are required. Some vendors—like Microsoft on Windows Phone 8—provide direct access to the device features using JavaScript without extra components.

The focus of this chapter is on the second approach only.

OS

A new OS version launch is always important from the hybrid application's view. As discussed earlier, hybrid applications are dependent on the webview component. If there are webview implementation changes in an OS upgrade, this impacts the hybrid application. How?

Webview components work on a default browser engine. The following is a sample mapping:

- Android based ➤ webview ➤ uses Chrome ➤ uses the WebKit engine

- iPhone based ➤ webview ➤ uses Safari ➤ uses the WebKit engine

- Windows Phone based ➤ webview ➤ uses IE ➤ uses the Trident engine

So, when there is a change in the browser due to updates or a new OS version launch, a hybrid application may require attention. Earlier iOS and Android never used the default browser's rendering engine as it is in a webview; rather, the engine or logic for the webview itself was different!

Back then, the performance difference for a hybrid application running in a webview vs. a default browser was considerable. Running a web application in the native browser was much faster than running the hybrid application in a webview.

In 2011, Facebook made a hybrid application. It was launched for iOS. But eventually, Facebook withdrew the application due to the slowdown of a UI webview-based rendering. Facebook later finalized a native approach.

Apple announced a WebKit-based rendering at the 2014 World Wide Developer Conference (WWDC). This forced hybrid application developers to do a check whether their app was running on iOS 8 (or above/below) before the application started. Developers continue to fear that "We can check version of iOS and verify that it's 8.0 or greater, but what if Apple removes WKWebKit in iOS 9?"

So the following code snippet (from `http://floatlearning.com`) is recommended for detecting the webview version:

```
if (NSClassFromString(@"WKWebView")) {
    _webView = [[WKWebView alloc] initWithFrame: [[self view] bounds]];
} else {
    _webView = [[UIWebView alloc] initWithFrame: [[self view] bounds]];
}
```

This code checks whether WKWebView is available on the current iOS, based on a non-OS element.

In 2014, Google announced the Android "Lollipop" version along with support for an updatable webview. This launch provided the boost required for hybrid application development. Since then, hybrid applications have been more consistent between devices and they give better performance. With this launch, Google also made remote debugging available for Android apps. More information is available at `https://developer.chrome.com/devtools/docs/remote-debugging`.

The following summarizes this discussion:

- Hybrid applications are now faster and even more recommended.

- While defining hybrid application around WKWebView, you have to consider the OS versions on which the application is going to work.

Let's discuss how the application framework or platform works for hybrid applications. We'll cover the core of hybrid application development: Apache Cordova.

Application Frameworks and Platforms

Apache Cordova is an open source hybrid mobile application framework. You can download it at `https://cordova.apache.org`.

The Apache Software Foundation launched Cordova in 2012. The entire code for a hybrid application based on Cordova is normally written in one single file named `index.html`. Cordova helps HTML and JavaScript code to work on webview. In order to access native features of the device, a plug-in is required.

As per Apache.org: "A plug-in is an interface available for Cordova and native components to communicate with each other." There are many third-party plug-ins available that can be downloaded and used in the project based on the functionality required. These plug-ins are mentioned in the plug-in registry at `http://cordova.apache.org/plug-ins/`. You can author your own plug-in with helper files offered by Apache at `https://cordova.apache.org/docs/en/5.1.1/guide/hybrid/plug-ins/index.html`.

Figure 5-2 lists core device features supported by core plug-ins in Cordova.

	Amazon-Fire OS	Android	Blackberry 10	Firefox OS	iOS	Ubuntu	Windows Phone 8	Windows 8.0, 8.1, Phone 8.1	Tizen
Cordova CLI	✓ Mac, Windows, Linux	✓ Mac, Windows, Linux	✓ Mac, Windows	✓ Mac, Windows, Linux	✓ Mac	✓ Ubuntu	✓ Windows Phone 8	✓	✗
Embedded WebView	✓	✓	✗	✗	✓	✓	✗	✗	✗
Plug-in Interface	✓	✓	✓	✗	✓	✓	✓	✓	✗
Platform APIs									
Accelerometer	✓	✓	✓	✓	✓	✓	✓	✓	✓
Battery Status	✓	✓	✓	✓	✓	X	✓	✓ Windows Phone 8.1 only	✓
Camera	✓	✓	✓	✓	✓	✓	✓	✓	✓
Capture	✓	✓	✓	✗	✓	✓	✓	✓	✗
Compass	✓	✓	✓	✗	✓	✓	✓	✓	✓
Connection	✓	✓	✓	✗	✓	✓	✓	✓	✓
Contacts	✓	✓	✓	✓	✓	✓	✓	partially	✗
Device	✓	✓	✓	✓	✓	✓	✓	✓	✓
Events	✓	✓	✓	✗	✓	✓	✓	✓	✓
File	✓	✓	✓	✗	✓	✓	✓	✓	✗
File Transfer	✓	✓	✓ Do not support on progress nor abort	✗	✓	✗	✓ Do not support on progress nor abort	✓ Do not support on progress nor abort	✗
Geolocation	✓	✓	✓	✓	✓	✓	✓	✓	✓
Globalization	✓	✓	✓	✗	✓	✓	✓	✓	✗
InAppBrowser	✓	✓	✓	✗	✓	✓	✓	Uses iFrame	✗
Media	✓	✓	✓	✗	✓	✓	✓	✓	✓
Notification	✓	✓	✓	✗	✓	✓	✓	✓	✓
Splashscreen	✓	✓	✓	✗	✓	✓	✓	✓	✗
Status Bar	✗	✓	✗	✗	✓	✗	✓	✓ Windows Phone 8.1 only	✓
Storage	✓	✓	✓	✗	✓	✓	✓ Local Storage & indexed DB	✓ Local Storage & indexed DB	✓
Vibration	✓	✓	✓	✓	✓	✗	✓	✓ Windows Phone 8.1 only	✗

Figure 5-2. *Core device features supported by Cordova core plug-ins (from* `https://cordova.apache.org`*)*

How Do Hybrid Applications Work on Devices?

A webview is very generic name given to a browser-like control by the mobile OS. This control is used by native applications when the application wants to load and show local web content on the device.

Normally, hybrid application developers exploit the webview control to load web content from a local or a remote server. To code, we use JavaScript—dynamic behavior and data loading happens through JavaScript. Please note that webviews render the UI using native browser context, which means Safari matters for the iPhone, Chrome matters for the Android, and IE for Windows Phone. The launch of a new SDK along with a webview directly affects hybrid applications. New updates are made available by vendors less frequently.

Why a webview and not the browser directly? Browsers restrict calls to devices. A webview is a native component offered by the platform. A webview can have access to other native components and libraries and indirectly access device features.

The difficult part to understand is how a hybrid application developed using HTML and JavaScript gets access to native device features. The short answer is "through a webview." The long answer is through the JavaScript calls made by the developer along with Cordova are intercepted by the webview. For example, JavaScript calls to a function like camera are converted into prompt commands, and then through JsBridge, with a webview, the actual camera can be accessed.

This is insane, as the mapping call from JavaScript to native may differ from vendor to vendor, like from Android to Apple. But, we are not concerned with this because Cordova does this brilliantly. Cordova has a lot of work already done.

Figure 5-3 describes the communication with native APIs using a webview. As you can see, a webview runs and hosts HTML5 and JavaScript code. Normally, HTML code is preferred in a single file. This means that multiple pages or views exist in the application and then a hide-show-div approach is preferred.

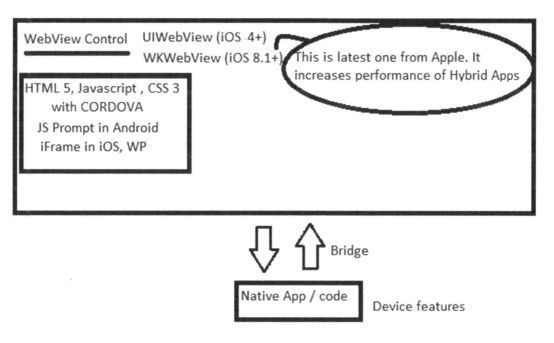

Figure 5-3. *Communication with native APIs using a webview*

The usage of multiple files through MV* (Model-View-*) design approach may make it difficult to maintain a state of the data while navigation takes place. In MV*, the * represents "Controller" or "Presenter" or a similar component.

A Cordova JavaScript file is always required in the project. The entire program is based on a configuration XML file that conveys to the webview information about the device features referred to in the program.

Consider our first hybrid application. What if we need to use a core or a custom plug-in on top of Cordova? Can we configure the same using Telerik AppBuilder?

Of course! We can customize references to the application using AppBuilder. If an application is created on Cordova version 2.X, then, by default, all the core plug-ins are referred to in the application. Using AppBuilder, you aren't able to modify the core plug-in architecture of the application.

However, if an application is created on Cordova 3.X, then enabling and disabling the plug-in is easily allowed through AppBuilder.

Kindly make a note that if you have several projects in the AppBuilder, then a plug-in addition is not global. These plug-ins need to be added individually in each project. Let's look at how this can be done.

1. Open our first hybrid application project, Apress Project, using AppBuilder in the browser client. Let's focus on Solution Explorer, as shown in Figure 5-4.

Figure 5-4. AppBuilder in Solution Explorer

We have a default reference to `cordova.js` in the project.

2. You can configure the plug-ins by double-clicking Properties. The location is highlighted in Figure 5-3. The configuration window is displayed, as shown in Figure 5-5. The highlighted portion denotes the availability of Cordova plug-in 3.X.

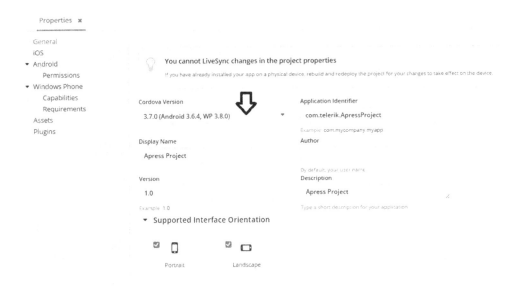

Figure 5-5. *Project configure properties*

As discussed earlier, you can customize (enable or disable) the core Cordova plug-ins if the application uses Cordova 3.X. This is normally done to minimize the deploy size as well as increase performance.

3. After clicking Properties, a configuration window appears (see Figure 5-6).

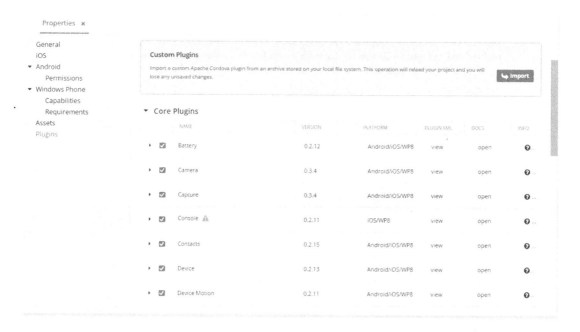

Figure 5-6. Cordova plug-ins

As you can see in Figure 5-6, custom plug-ins can be installed by importing.

Plug-ins from the marketplace can also be installed and used in an application. The core plug-ins are shown in Figure 5-6. Marketplace plug-ins are shown in Figure 5-7.

▼ Other Plugins

⊕ Install from Plugins Marketplace

	NAME	VERSION	PLATFORM	PLUGIN XML	DOCS	INFO
▸ ☐	Telerik Analytics	3.3.1	Android/iOS/WP8	view	open	❷...
▸ ☐	Telerik AppFeedback	1.4	Android/iOS	view	open	❷...
▸ ☐	Telerik Mobile Testing	2.4.0.3	Android/iOS/WP8	view	open	❷...

Figure 5-7. Marketplace plug-ins

You don't need to manually add any entries for core plug-ins in `index.html` and `config.XML`.

4. After enabling or disabling the required plug-ins, add or remove any third-party plug-ins.
    You can continue to use the AppBuilder as you did in the first hybrid application.

Some plug-ins may be vendor-specific. An example for storing data securely in local storage you can use iOS Keychain plug-in. It can be downloaded from `http://plug-ins.telerik.com/cordova/plug-in/keychain`.

It is always suggested to keep reference of those plug-ins that are required and used by a hybrid application. Remove whatever is nonsense and is not required.

Due to security flaws, avoid Android "Gingerbread" as a targeted OS. (More on this at `http://www.techworm.net`.)

If you want to load or show remote unknown contents into the app, using the in-browser plug-in is suggested. It loads remote contents using the native browser's security model, restricting access to resources on the machine.

A list of well-known plug-ins is available at `http://cordova.apache.org/docs/en/edge/cordova/plug-ins/plug-inapis.html`.

Webview Hybrid Limitations

A webview in a hybrid application may surprise you with its strange behavior. Let's look at the example of embedding video inside a hybrid application. You can use an HTML5-specific video tag. However, if you use iFrame to load a YouTube video, then it may render the video content outside the container. The memory required while using iFrame is on the high side. This kind of issue is considered a behavior on iOS.

Another problem is that while referring contents from a local file, memory usage can be on the higher side. On an iPad, you may use an iPad-based web server to get the content like `CocoaHTTPServer`. It can be downloaded from `https://github.com/robbiehanson/CocoaHTTPServer`.

Comparison: Native vs. Hybrid Applications

Table 5-1 is compares native and hybrid applications, listing only the core working architecture of either application type. The + and the – denote comparatively better or less favorable, respectively. These comparisons may help you choose between a native and a hybrid application.

***Table 5-1.** Native vs. Hybrid Applications*

Point	Native	Hybrid	Explanation
Performance	+	–	A native app executes directly under the context of the device OS. It may use a webview to load remote mark-up content.
			However, an HTML-based hybrid app is always dependent on usage of a webview.
Direct access to device's feature	+	–	A native app gets access and helper libraries to access device-specific features.
			A hybrid app needs a plug-in.
UI	+	–	Vendor acceptable UI is easy to create in a native app. Mimicking a native UI into a hybrid is difficult. Example: Table cells in iPhone native apps are difficult to replace in hybrid applications.
Communication with Server	–	+	Native APIs can help communicate with the server using well-known protocols along with security.
			Hybrid applications communicate with the server using XML-HTTP or AJAX. JSON data transfer can be done. But, if you consider enterprise applications, they communicate with the server through the Web. This means that we are not considering data stored on the device; we are considering data being transferred.
Local Data Security	+	–	Hybrid applications rely on third-party plug-ins
Touch delays	+	–	If hybrid applications use WebKitView, then it adds a considerable amount of delay (~200ms) in handling touch.

However, if you consider the following factors, hybrid applications are far better in these aspects.

- Cost of development
- Time to market the application
- Resources availability in the market
- Reusability of the code
- Plug-in availability

Summary

This chapter discussed the importance of the *webview* and how hybrid applications work. It also focused on the Cordova plug-in, on top of which many plug-ins are built. Finally, it compared hybrid and native applications from the perspective of internals.

The next chapter discusses data access techniques in hybrid applications.

CHAPTER 6

■ ■ ■

Data Access in HMAD

The objectives of this chapter are to

- Learn ways to transfer data between the client mobile application and the server

- Learn ways to securely pass data

- Learn how to use tools to monitor the network and the data

- Learn different data formats

This chapter discusses data access in hybrid mobile applications and service-oriented architecture. The major focus is on accessing JSON and XML data in hybrid application(s) through web services and Windows Communication Foundation (WCF) Service. We also discuss ways to secure this communication. Let's start by discussing various ways to transfer data.

Exploring Data Access Possibilities

If we consider only server-side endpoints to transfer data, there are many options available from Microsoft, .NET, Java, and PHP. As discussed earlier, for hybrid applications, it does not matter which server-side technology or tools you use. As long as the server returns data to the client application in an understandable and well-known format—such as JSON, XML, String, or Arrays—the client side is always happy.

Tables 6-1, 6-2, and 6-3 list the technology and languages provided for data access on the server side.

Table 6-1. *Microsoft: Data Access on the Server Side*

(+/-)	HTTP Handler	Web Services	Windows Communication Foundation (WCF) and REST	Web APIs/Controllers
(+)points	Easiest way available to transfer data. Always hosted on a web server. With the help of generic handler using Microsoft.NET, you can decide the content type to be returned from the server. When data is passed from hybrid mobile application using AJAX; if it is GET request then it can collected on server using query string. If it is POST request then it can be collected on server using InputStream.	Oldest and easiest way available to transfer data. Always hosted on a web server. Default protocol used is universally accepted as Simple Object Access Protocol (i.e., SOAP). Internally, data is always passed in XML format over HTTP. Data entities are created from data passed automatically by SOAP deserialization process. Data in XML form is default way.	Extended compared to handlers and web services. Hosted on web server, COM+ server. Also can be self-hosted. Well-known protocols can be used in communication using TCP, HTTP, UDP, P2P, etc. However, we will use HTTP only. Data serialization is decided based on the protocol. For example, it is binary when TCP; SOAP when HTTP. Data entities are created from data passed automatically. JSON data format along with Representational State Transfer (REST) is also supported.	Newest way of data transfer. Always hosted on web server. HTTP protocol is carrier. Data can be passed in the form of XML / JSON. Data entities are created from data passed automatically.
(–) points	Generic handlers with extension "ASHX" is quickest way to do so. However, security of data is programmer's concern and needs to be provided using security APIs in .NET. Managed objects (like in C#) are not constructed automatically from the data received. Handlers can be called by any client like hybrid application, web, desktop application, etc.; but using HTTP carrier only.	Again, data security is provided through APIs like SOAP headers and extensions. Web services can be called by any client like hybrid application, web, desktop application, etc.; but using HTTP carrier only.	IIS is considered a default web server host. It by default supports HTTP protocol. TCP support was added after IIS 7.5 onward. Many data security APIs exist. Self-hosting is more complex compared to IIS hosting.	This requires ASP.NET MVC infrastructure. Data security is provided through APIs.

Let's look at sample code snippets. All code snippets assume that we need to transfer the Employee class object from server side to client.

```
// comments added in the code denotes important statement
Employee class layout is like:
public class Employee
{
    public int No { get; set; }
    public string Name {  get; set; }
    public string Address { get; set; }
}
```

The code snippet for the handler:

```
//Code is written in file with .ASHX extension
public class TestHandler : IHttpHandler
    {
        public void ProcessRequest(HttpContext context)
        {
          //IMPORTANT: One can set contentType in the following line:
            context.Response.ContentType = "application/json";
            JavaScriptSerializer jss = new JavaScriptSerializer();
            context.Response.Write(jss.Serialize(new Employee()));
        }

        public bool IsReusable{ get{ return false; }}
    }
```

The code snippet for web services:

```
// Code is written in file with .ASMX extension
 [Webservice]    //This line conveys this class is available for call remotely
public class TestWebService
{
  [Webmethod]    //This line conveys; that this method is available for calling
  public Employee GetEmployee()
  {
    return new Employeee();
  }
}
```

Code snippet for WCF services:

```
//Code is written in file with .SVC extension
//The following line conveys that implementation of this interface
//is available for call remotely
[ServiceContract]
```

```
public interface ITestWCFService
{
   //The following line conveys; that method implementation is available for calling
   [OperationContract]
   Employee GetEmployee()
}

//The following is actual implementation of an interface inside class
public class TestWCFService:ITestWCFService
{
  public Employee GetEmployee()
  {
     return new Employeee();
  }
}
```

The code snippet for the Web API controller in ASP.NET MVC:

```
// Code is written in plain code file (eg. C# files like .cs extension)
// APIController is base class offered by ASP.NET MVC Framework
public class ValuesController:ApiController
{
 //While calling The following method; use url like - "http://<server>/api/values/<id>"
 //GET conveys that only "GET" requests can reach to this method
  public Employee Get (int id)
  {
     return new Employeee();
  }
}
```

Table 6-2. *Java / Oracle: Data Access on Server Side*

(+/–)	Servlet	Web Services
(+)points	Easiest option available for data transfer.	Old and easy option available for data transfer.
	Content type of the response can be set manually.	Data is always passed using SOAP format. Internally uses XML over Http
	You can even set it to XML / JSON.	Plain Old Java Objects are formed automatically while data is received from client. Conversion tools like JaxB, JiBX can be used to create POJO.
	GET, POST request data can be collected using QueryString and getParameter() method respectively	
	This can be clubbed with any back-end business logic written using EJB or any legacy code!	Deserialization part is handled automatically.
		Host is web server.
	Host is web server.	REST is supported through REST APIs; also known as JAX-RS
(–) points	Only HTTP carrier can be used	Only HTTP carrier can be used.
	Security of data is not automatically given; rather provided through Java APIs	Data security is applied through code.
	Primarily used for HTML like output generation.	

The code snippet for servlet returning employee's data in JSON format:

```
public class TestServlet extends HttpServlet {
 protected void doGet(HttpServletRequest request,
        HttpServletResponse response)
 {
        //set contentType to anything here. The following code sets up type to 'json'
        response.setContentType("application/json");

        // The following, employee related data is written in JSON format
        // One may use custom code for achieving the same or
        // use 'jsonobject' class
        response.getWriter().write("{Name:'James',Address:'London'}");
 }

 protected void doPost(HttpServletRequest request,
        HttpServletResponse response)
        // TODO Auto-generated method stub
        doGet(request, response);
    }
}
```

The code snippet for Java web service endpoint using the Java API for XML Web Services (JAX-WS):

```
import javax.jws.WebService;

//The following code '@Webservice conveys that the code open for call remotely
@WebService
public class TestWebService
{
    //The following code '@WebMethod' conveys that the method is open for call remotely
    @WebMethod
    public Employee GetEmployee() {
        return new Employee();
    }
}
```

Table 6-3. *PHP: Data Access on Server Side*

(+/–)	PHP Page Using Content Type
(+)points	Easiest option available for data transfer.
	Web server is a host.
	Content type of the response can be set to anything including XML / JSON.
	REST support can be added optionally.
	PUT and DELETE request complex implementation needs to be handled.
(–)points	Only HTTP carrier.
	Data security needs to be provided through code.

The code snippet for the PHP endpoint using content type JSON:

```php
<?php
    //The following line conveys about content type being returned from PHP
    header("Content-Type:application/json");

    //return employee data
    echo   '{"No":1,"Name":"sachin","Address":"mumbai"}';
?>
```

Data Serialization Techniques

Usually, data can be easily transferred in the form of XML or JSON from the server side by simply setting the content type. However, in an earlier section, we discussed many ways to achieve the same. At a high level, if we try to categories most the techniques, we see two groups:

- SOAP-based communication

- REST-based communication

What is the difference between the two? What are the advantages and disadvantages of each? Let's look at this now.

SOAP is the default protocol for accessing web services. It's been in the technology market for a while. SOAP was developed by Microsoft. SOAP is a bit difficult to use in some languages, while in others, it's a piece of cake. SOAP relies completely on XML to transfer data. Microsoft's goal in developing the SOAP protocol was to replace older technologies that don't work well on the Internet; an example of such a technology is Distributed Component Object Model (DCOM).

After launching the first draft of SOAP, Microsoft handed over the details to a community called the Internet Engineering Task Force (IETF), where it was standardized and made open to the technology world. Many standards were built around SOAP afterward, such as WS-Policy and WS-ReliableMessaging, and so forth.

SOAP-based web services also completely rely on a concept called Web Service Description Language (WSDL), which is a file that contains all the information any client ever requires to call the service. This information includes information such as where to call, how to call, and what data to pass on.

A call to SOAP-based services through JavaScript is difficult. The formation of a request in JavaScript with XML is not handy at all. If the response comes in the form of XML, then before DOM version 2, very difficult and nonstandard ways of dealing with XML were used. What happened in DOM2? We got an extra object, since then called XmlHttpRequest [XHR], along with documents, Windows, and Navigator into the DOM tree. So, compared to SOAP, which relies on XML, REST simply relies on URL.

REST is new to the market compared to SOAP. A call can be given to the server using a REST URL, but you have to use the HTTP 1.1 verbs GET, POST, PUT, and DELETE. SOAP web services only use XML, whereas REST uses different data formats, including JSON, RSS (Really Simple Syndication) feeds along with XML.

So, what you should you prefer: SOAP or REST? The consultant's answer is—It depends!

The decision depends on many factors, such as the following:

- The technology used on the server side and whether it supports REST (being new)

- The technology used on the client side

- Whether the client understands JSON or XML

- The protocol used for communication

- And more

Tips to GET or SET Data

To pass data between the client and the server, two techniques or verbs are used very frequently: GET and POST. Other —like DELETE, PUT, and HEAD—are not as frequently used because they have specific purposes.

As HTTP is a protocol, data travels in packets. A packet has a header and a body. If the data travels in the header, then it's a GET request. If the data travels in the body, then it's a POST request. POST is safe compared to GET, because GET data can be seen in the URL.

Table 6-4 is a basic comparison between GET and POST requests.

Table 6-4. *GET and POST Comparison*

GET	POST
• Data entered travels in the header part of the HTTP	• Data entered travels in the body part of the HTTP
• Data can be seen in the URL itself, so not safe.	• Data cannot be seen directly. However, with the tools like fiddler it can be seen.
• This method should not be used to transfer critical data	• This method is generally used to transfer critical data like username and password
• Only ASCII data is allowed to be passed	• No restrictions
• If one does refresh the page or hits back button, then it does not cause any harm	• If one does refresh the page or hits back button; then it does re submit the content
• Contents passed using this method is allowed for caching	• Contents passed using this method does not get cached
• Data + URL <= 2048 characters	• Generally, a maximum size of 4GB is recommended.

Let's look at certain tools that help debug and test client-side code. We will use the hybrid application developed in Chapter 4 as a base for debugging and testing.

1. Start the Visual studio editor.

2. Click File Menu ➤ Open ➤ File.

3. A file opens and a dialog box appears.

4. Browse to the `<local drive>\Apress\CH04\HelloClient` folder.

5. Select index.html from the folder and click Open.

The content looks like what is shown in Figure 6-1.

Figure 6-1. *Open first HMAD project*

6. Make sure that there is still a reference to live server-side code, such as
   `http://bonaventuresystems.com/Apress/BeginningHMAD/CH04/SayHello.ashx`.

7. Run this file using the F5 key to check whether it still works.

Output like what's shown in Figure 6-2 must appear in the open default browser.

Figure 6-2. *Recheck the code*

Now, that we are sure that the code is still working, let's test network traffic with tools such as the browser's built-in helper and Telerik Fiddler.

1. Enter the URL for the index page (see Figure 6-2) in the Google Chrome browser.

2. Press Ctrl+Shift+i or press the F12 key. This action opens UI Developer Tools
   (see Figure 6-3).

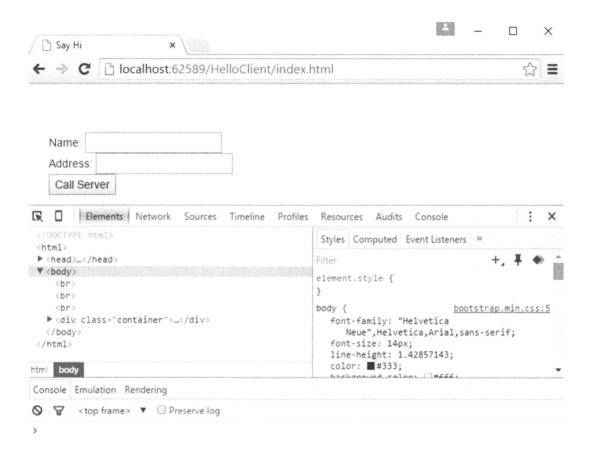

Figure 6-3. *Developer Tools in Chrome*

    3.   In the Developer Tools, click the Network tab, as shown in Figure 6-4.

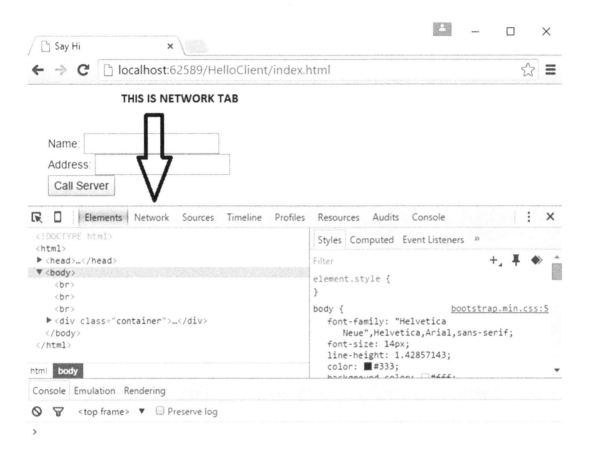

Figure 6-4. *Developer Tool: Network*

4. Refresh the index.html page by pressing Ctrl+F5.

5. Note the change in the Network tab.

The Network tab displays downloadable resources, like JQuery and Bootstrap files; without these resources, index.html cannot function. The Network tab also displays other information (see Figure 6-5).

Figure 6-5. *Developer Tools: Network*

6. As shown in the Figure 6-5, you can click a specific request to see more details.

7. To test, click the index.html entry listed. All entries are mentioned in Figure 6-5.

More details are shown in Figure 6-6.

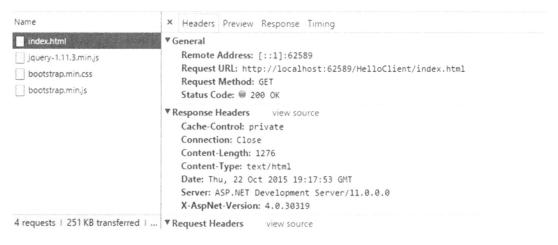

Figure 6-6. *Developer Tools: Request details*

8. Make a note of the request method mentioned as GET

9. From the response header, it is clear that output received is of type text/html.

10. The details also contain who returned this output; this conveys which technology the server has used.

11. Note the content-length specified.

12. Look at the response and preview details. It shows more markup and the HTML source, as shown in Figures 6-7 and 6-8.

Figure 6-7. *Developer Tools: Response and Preview details*

Figure 6-8. *Developer Tools: Time tab*

You can get more information on where the delay is in entire cycle of request and reply. At this time, if someone clicks the Call Server button, one more request is added in the pool on the left side (see Figure 6-9).

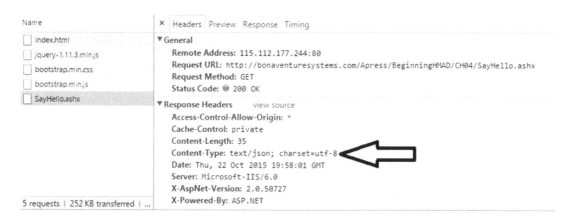

Figure 6-9. *Developer Tools: New request on Call ServerClick*

Now, if you want to see the response contents, click the Response tab. It shows data in JSON format, as shown in Figure 6-10.

Name	× Headers Preview Response Timing
☐ index.html	1 {"Name":"James","Address":"London"}
☐ jquery-1.11.3.min.js	
☐ bootstrap.min.css	
☐ bootstrap.min.js	
☐ SayHello.ashx	

Figure 6-10. *Developer Tools: JSON after GET*

In Figure 6-11, a call to SayHello.ashx was made as a GET call using AJAX.

```
$.ajax({
    url: 'http://bonaventuresystems.com/Apress/BeginningHMAD/CH04/SayHello.ashx',
    type: 'GET',              explicit call using GET
    success: function (result)
    {
        $('#txtName').val(result.Name);
        $('#txtAddress').val(result.Address);
    },
    error: function (err) { alert('Error!'); }
});
```

Figure 6-11. *Developer Tools: Explicit GET AJAX Call*

What will happen if we make the same changes to POST? The results are shown in Figure 6-12. Data passed (if any) travels in the body of the HTTP packet. As you can see in Figure 6-12, nothing changes except the request method as POST. Pulling data out of the body is automatically done by the browser. The browser first dissects the content type and then decides what to do with it.

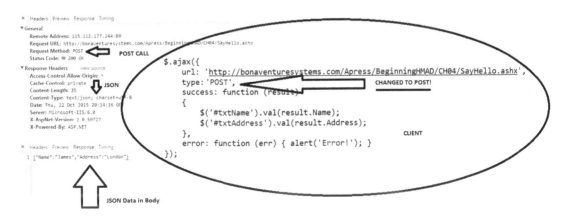

Figure 6-12. *Developer Tools: Explicit POST AJAX Call*

113

You can also use Telerik Fiddler to the do the same job. However, it is more advanced than the default supplied browser-based developer tools. Telerik Fiddler can help to generate a request to do tests only. You may even dissect HTTPS details to a certain extent with the help of Telerik Fiddler.

Let's use Fiddler and have a glimpse.

1. Download free copy of Fiddler at `http://www.telerik.com/fiddler`.

2. Do the step-by-step installation procedure. After installation, start Fiddler. The default fiddler UI looks like what's shown in Figure 6-13.

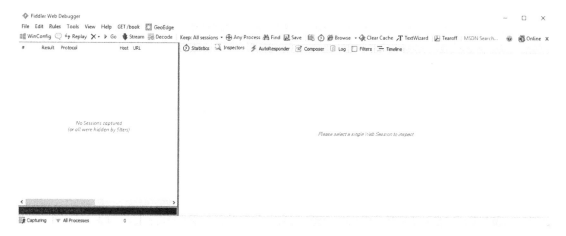

Figure 6-13. *Telerik Fiddler*

3. Open Google Chrome and start browsing index.html, as shown in Figure 6-2. Note the call to index.html and the dependent resources being tracked, as shown in Figure 6-14.

#	Result	Protocol	Host	URL	Body	Caching	Content-Type	Process
1	200	HTTP	localhost:62589	/HelloClient/index.html	1,277	private	text/html	chrome:9136
2	200	HTTP	localhost:62589	/HelloClient/jquery-1.11.3...	95,957	private	application/...	chrome:9136
3	200	HTTP	localhost:62589	/HelloClient/bootstrap.min...	122,540	private	text/css	chrome:9136
4	200	HTTP	localhost:62589	/HelloClient/bootstrap.min.js	36,816	private	application/...	chrome:9136

Figure 6-14. *Telerik Fiddler: default session tracking*

4. Switch back to Google Chrome and click the Call Server button. Notice the changes in the request and response header. Observe the same in Figure 6-15. Keep it in mind that we are tracking an AJAX call through external components.

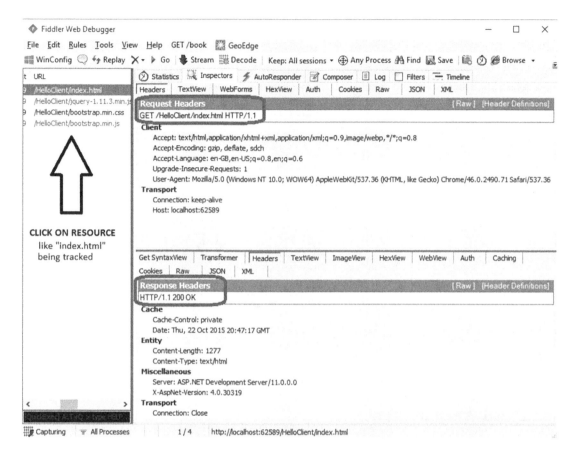

Figure 6-15. Telerik Fiddler: AJAX call being tracked

So far, we have used Fiddler for tracking the calls over network. We can also use fiddler for raising different kind of requests as if client.

5.   Select the Composer tab. Do the actions shown in Figure 6-16.

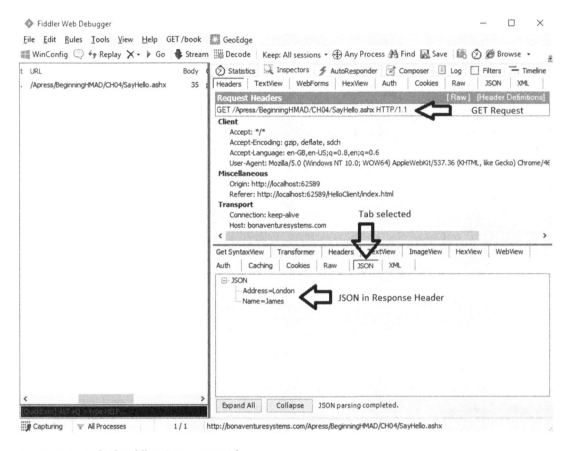

Figure 6-16. Telerik Fiddler: Composer window

6. From the Composer window, select POST as the request type. Enter the index.
    html URL at the location indicated by an arrow. Click the Execute button.
    This action takes you back to the Inspectors window (see Figure 6-17).

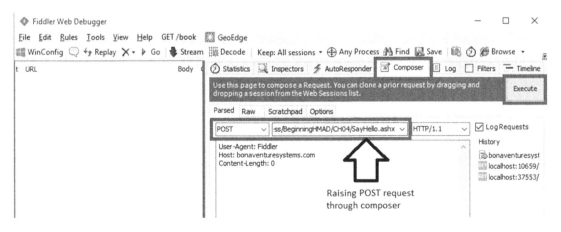

Figure 6-17. Telerik Fiddler: Inspectors window

This is similar to when we explicitly offered a POST call to server. By using Composer, we can save a lot of time when testing calls to the server over multiple verbs.

Browser-based Debug, Monitor, and Trace

Debugging is needed to find logical errors in code. For managed code like C#, Java editors provide very rich support for debugging. However, JavaScript remains ignored by many editors. Today, browsers do have extended support for debugging JavaScript. Let's look at the support given by Google Chrome. Similar support is provided by other browsers.

Let's use our first hybrid mobile application to learn about debugging.

1. Browse index.html to the Google Chrome browser.

2. Make sure that code for the Call Server button click is still working.

3. Open the code for index.html in Visual Studio.

4. Add a debugger to the AJAX code inside index.html, as shown in Figure 6-18.

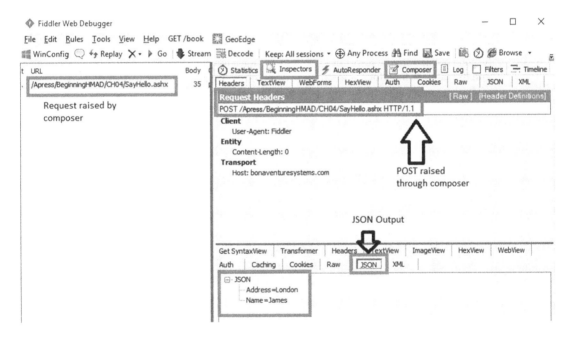

Figure 6-18. *Add debugger inside JavaScript code*

5. Open Developer Tools. Press the F12 key on the keyboard or click the Customize and Control Google Chrome button in the right corner of the address bar. Select More tools ➤ Developer Tools.

6. Once the Developer Tools are open, the Chrome browser looks like what's shown in Figure 6-19.

Figure 6-19. *Google Chrome with Developer Tools*

7. Click the Call Server button. Based on whether the response is successful or not, the code breaks into the respective function. We have the debugger added in both the callback functions—on success and on error. As seen in Figure 6-20, the call back is successful and the code pauses in the success function.

Figure 6-20. *Debugger in success function*

8. You can check the values received from the server by querying through the Console window. Open the Console window using the Console tab (see Figure 6-21) .

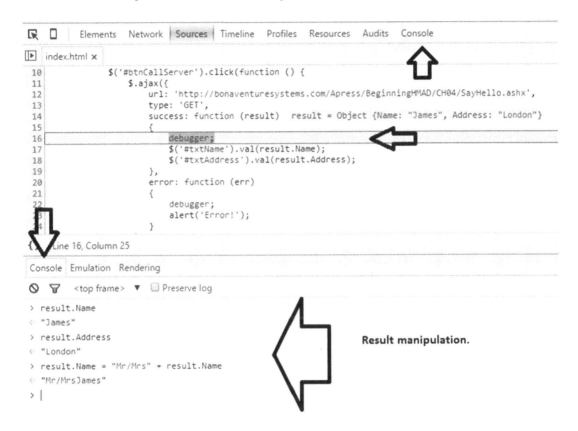

Figure 6-21. Result manipulation using Console window

9. Query to the result variable and manipulate the same based on the need.

10. After all the changes mentioned in Figure 6-21 are done, click the Resume Script Execution button (visible in the index.html) or press F8 to continue the execution (see Figure 6-22).

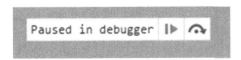

Figure 6-22. Resume Script Execution

Changes to the result received can be observed in UI (see Figure 6-23).

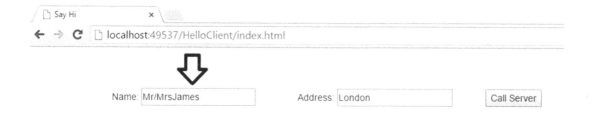

Figure 6-23. *UI after result manipulation*

Similarly, you can debug and manipulate with Firefox, IE (EDGE), and other browsers.

Code and Data Security

Now let's discuss another important concept in hybrid mobile applications. For hybrid apps, UI testing can be easily done with the help of browsers only. It is preferable that the code be written in JavaScript or JQuery. The deployable output in Android and Windows Phone hybrid applications is an internally compressed file. You can uncompress and find internal files like index.html. Afterward, finding JavaScript or JQuery code inside the index.html file is not tough.

Similar issuess are faced by web programmers when most of the code is written in JavaScript. Since JavaScript runs on the browser, you can read the JavaScript code contents by viewing the source.

How to protect JavaScript code? Two options exist:

- Do not provide the entire code. Load the JavaScript in pieces. Download pieces from the server side on demand. The benefit is that it becomes difficult to understand the entire functionality in one go.

- Obfuscate and minify JavaScript code with the help of obfuscation and bundling tools.

Providing JavaScript files or resources on demand is a feature of server side and custom logic. However, obfuscation and minification of JavaScript can be done through tools. Let's talk about the frequently used tools for minification:

- JSMIN by Mr. Douglas Crockford (well known for JSON).

    - JSMIN can be downloaded from `http://www.crockford.com`.

    - As per crockford.com, JSMIN minimizes the JavaScript contents and makes it difficult to read. It is not for obfuscation.

- Google Closure Compiler

    - This is a called a compiler yet it compiles JavaScript code to better JavaScript. It's a program written in Java.

    - It does parse and minify JavaScript.

    - Download it from `https://developers.google.com/closure/compiler/`.

- YUI Compressor

    - A code compressor from Yahoo!. It's a command-line utility developed using Java.

    - It can be downloaded from http://yui.github.io/yuicompressor/.

- ShrinkSafe: DOJO Toolkit

    - A code compressor from DOJO. It is a utility developed on Java.

    - Offline version at http://svn.dojotoolkit.org/src/util/trunk/shrinksafe/shrinksafe.jar.

    - Online version can be referred from http://shrinksafe.dojotoolkit.org.

To demonstrate what minification means, consider the following JavaScript code and store it in the sample.js file because it may be asked as an input by the compressor. Figure 6-24 explains.

```javascript
//This is comment is Javascript
//Another comment
//Yet another comment

//Below function does nothing!
function myfunction() {
    var v1 = 100;
    var v2 = new Date();
    var v3 = "some string";

    //Below is loop for no reason

    for (var i = 0; i < 100; i++) {
        document.writeln("For no reason " + i + " time(s)");

        //below is comparison for no reason

        if (i==20) {
            document.writeln("This is condition satisfied");
        }
    }

    //Call below function for no reason
    Second();

}

function Second() {
    alert('Hi, for no reason');
}
```

Figure 6-24. *Sample page*

1. Now visit http://shrinksafe.dojotoolkit.org, which is the online version of ShrinkSafe. ShrinkSafe's web page user interface is shown in Figure 6-25.

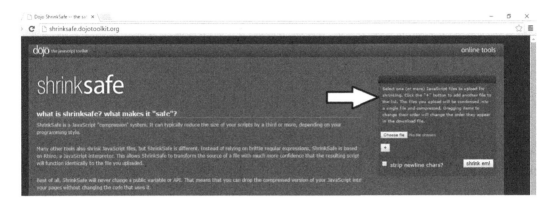

Figure 6-25. *ShrinkSafe web page*

2. As highlighted in the Figure 6-25, click Choose file. The browser file dialog box will appear.

3. Browser to the sample.js file created earlier.

4. Click Shrink em! This shrinks the contents from the sample.js file and automatically downloads the compressed file.

JavaScript obfuscation is a process through which we make JavaScript unreadable! This protects your code and prevents it from being stolen. The obfuscation process is done through a utility called the Obfuscator. While doing obfuscation, some obfuscators shrink the size of the JavaScript, which makes the JavaScript code download faster. So, obfuscation does many good things.

There are many obfuscators available on the market. To demonstrate the process, let's consider the following JavaScript code snippet from a case study appended after last chapter in this book. Save this script in the sample.js file. The code snippet size on disk is 932 bytes.

```
var modulesSize = $(jsonResult.survey.Modules.Module).size();
for (modulescnt = 0; modulescnt < modulesSize; modulescnt++) {
                 moduleData = null;
                 if (modulesSize == 1) {
             moduleData = jsonResult.survey.Modules.Module;
                 }
                 else {
             moduleData =  jsonResult.survey.Modules.Module[modulescnt];
                 }
                 ModuleText = moduleData.ModuleText[0].value;
                 ItemsCount = null;
                 ItemsData = null;
                 ItemsCount = $(moduleData.Items).size();
                 for (itemscnt = 0; itemscnt < ItemsCount; itemscnt++) {
                     if (ItemsCount == 1) {
                         ItemsData = moduleData.Items;
                     }
```

```
                                else {
                                    ItemsData = moduleData.Items[itemscnt];
                                }
                    }}
```

Now, let's do the obfuscation.

As discussed earlier, there are many obfuscators, such as JScrambler and Jasob. You must pay for most of these tools. The price varies from $30 to $50 annually. However, we will evaluate it through a trial edition. Let's use JSOB obfuscator.

1. Go to `http://www.butterflyfile.com/jasob-javascript-obfuscator`.

2. Click the Download Now button. This action downloads jsob.exe.

3. Install it on your Windows machine. During installation, please use the trial option.

4. After installation, start Jasob using the shortcut on the desktop or by browsing through the program files.

5. The UI appears as shown in Figure 6-26.

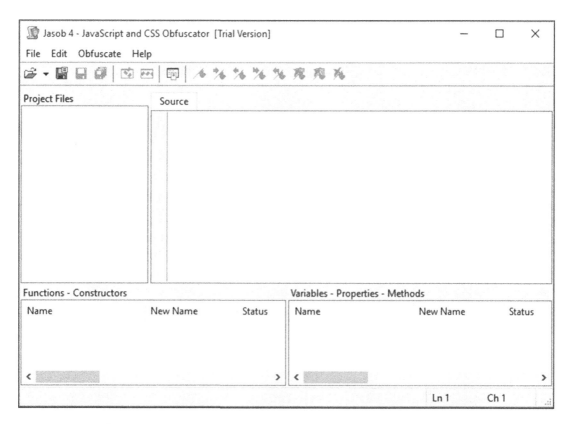

Figure 6-26. Jasob JavaScript Obfuscator

6.   Select File ➤ Open. This action opens a dialog box.

7.   Using the Open dialog box, browse to sample.js file ➤ Select. Click Open.

8.   Click Analyze Source Files, as shown in Figure 6-27.

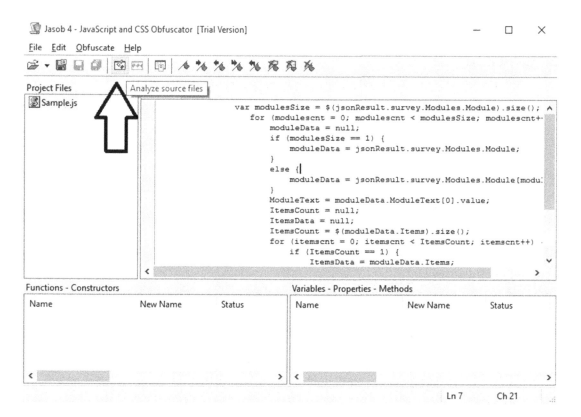

Figure 6-27. *Jasob: analyze source file*

This analyzes variables, which are lines that can be reduced and further obfuscated. More details can be observed in Figure 6-28. Also note that the Obfuscate Source File button is now activated.

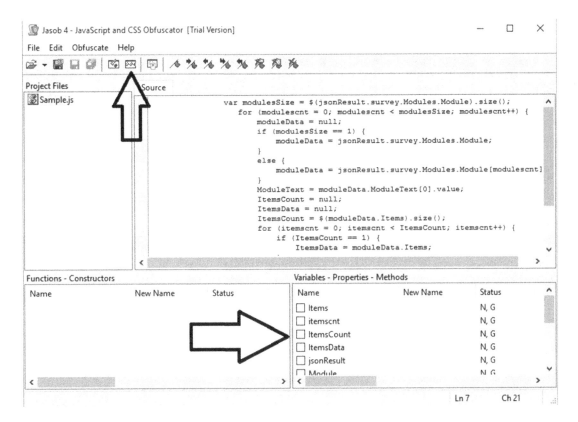

Figure 6-28. *Jasob: analyze and obfuscate source file*

9. Now, click the Obfuscate Source File button.

10. This obfuscates the sample.js contents and opens them in the Obfuscated tab (see Figure 6-29).

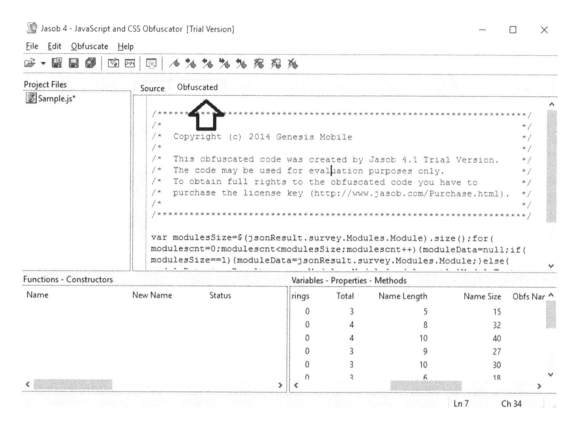

Figure 6-29. *Jasob after obfuscation*

After obfuscation, the code looks like this:

```
Code Snippet: Size of the code on disk = 509 bytes
-----------------------------------------------------------------------
var modulesSize=$(jsonResult.survey.Modules.Module).size();for(modulescnt=0;modulescn
t<modulesSize;modulescnt++){moduleData=null;if(modulesSize==1){moduleData=jsonResult.
survey.Modules.Module;}else{moduleData=jsonResult.survey.Modules.Module[modulescnt];}
ModuleText=moduleData.ModuleText[0].value;ItemsCount=null;ItemsData=null;ItemsCount=
$(moduleData.Items).size();for(itemscnt=0;itemscnt<ItemsCount;itemscnt++){if(ItemsCount==1)
{ItemsData=moduleData.Items;}else{ItemsData=moduleData.Items[itemscnt];}}}
-----------------------------------------------------------------------
    var modulesSize = $(jsonResult.survey.Modules.Modul
```

If you notice, the size of the code has drastically reduced to 509 bytes from 932 bytes and has no or less readability. So, using minification and obfuscation, we can successfully make JavaScript secure with a lower size. Obfuscation can protect code, but it may not help in the security of data, which comes dynamically from the UI.

How do we securely pass data to and from the server? There are multiple ways:

- HTTPS: Use Secure HTTP for data transfer. With HTTPS, it indirectly becomes the browser's responsibility to pass data securely. The job of checking a server's authenticity belongs to the browser. The typical steps followed in HTTPS communication are noted in Figure 6-30.

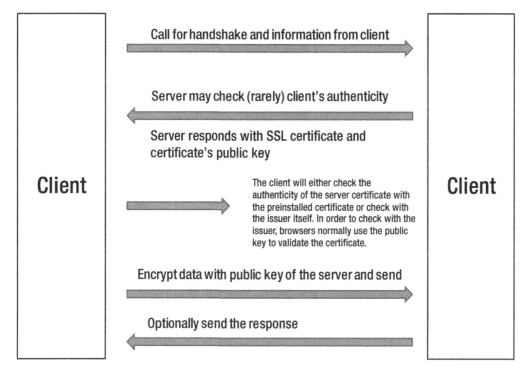

Figure 6-30. *HTTPS communication*

- HTTPS is always recommended for critical data transfer.
    - Obscure security mechanism (i.e., a complete custom approach like assembling data in a way it won't be understood easily while passed from and to the server. Customization may need lot of code. However, this approach is not recommended for very critical data.
    - Data hashing algorithm like Message Digest Ver.5 (MD5) or Secure Hash Algorithm Ver. 1 (SHA1)

- This is an integrity check algorithm. Data is passed along with the hash code. The other end checks data integrity by applying similar algorithms and then by comparing the old hash against the new hash.

- No direct implementation exists for MD5 or SHA1in JavaScript. However, you can code for the same or evaluate and use helper libraries given by:

  ```
  > Joseph Myers (http://www.myersdaily.org/joseph/javascript/md5-text.html)
  > Paul Johnston
  (http://pajhome.org.uk/crypt/md5/)
  > Masanao Izumo
  (https://gist.github.com/dsc/2970392)
  ```

- Token-based approach: Send a time-based token to the client in the initial response and validate the client against some calculations received back.

For credentials (like the username and password, which needs to be passed to server), the usage of a POST request is always advised.

Encode or encrypt? Many people get confused about these terms. The purpose of encoding data is to transform data in such a way that the data-receiving party can understand it. Keep it in mind, encoding never assures security. ASCII, binary, and Unicode are forms of encoding.

Encryption, however, makes data secure.

Summary

This chapter discussed the different ways available to transfer data in a hybrid mobile applications. We also learned the basics of GET and POST request.

The next chapter discusses responsive CSS and related style classes.

CHAPTER 7

■ ■ ■

UI for HMAD

The objectives of this chapter are to

- Learn about UI creation using JavaScript and JQuery
- Learn about the event handling mechanism in JQuery
- Learn about jQuery plug-ins to generate UI dynamically
- Learn about UI effects
- Learn about responsive UI style classes

This chapter looks at dynamic UI generation, JQuery plug-ins for UI manipulation, and the CSS classes for making a UI responsive.

HTML with JQuery

We already created a basic application in Chapter 4. We used very basic and static UI. Dynamically generating a user interface is not a complex task. You just need a container control (like div or section) and then programmatically find the container and append the HTML contents as a string.

When it comes to finding dynamically added controls or handling events for dynamically added controls, however, it is a complex job to accomplish. Why? Because handling events for the controls already known to the DOM tree is easy. When a control is added to the HTML <body> dynamically, then the new control's availability needs to be conveyed to the DOM tree first.

Let's consider a very general scenario. A hybrid mobile application pulls data from a server based on the certain filter conditions. To represent data, you can't suggest having a static hard-coded UI because the data is dynamic. This means that a mobile app doesn't know the amount of data it is going to receive. Hence, the application has to generate the UI dynamically, based on the size of the data.

Let's consider that the data is a set of records with fields like Name and Address in each record.

Now, in a dynamic UI, you want to show the container <DIV> based on the number of records received. Also each <DIV> should also have a <button> dynamically added. On click of each <button>, it should show "alert" with a "Hi" message and the respective person's name appended; for example, the message is "Hi James", on click of the button in the <DIV>, which has "James" written in one of the controls inside <DIV>.)

Let's build a solution considering the approach taken in Chapter 4. Let's now consider the code authored in SayHello.ashx.

The following steps make the changes in SayHello.ashx.

1. Open the HelloServer project.

   Make changes in the Person class. Add an extra No property of the integer type .final Person class will look like this:

   ```
   public class Person
    {
        public int No { get; set; }
        public string Name { get; set; }
        public string Address { get; set; }
    }
   ```

   Now, open SayHello.ashx. Make the following changes in the SayHello class, as highlighted in Figure 7-1.

2. Recall the cross origin issue discussed in Chapter 4. To solve this, let's add the following line (keep it as is).

   ```
   context.Response.AppendHeader("Access-Control-Allow-Origin", "*");
   ```

3. Compile the code and publish the code, as done in Chapter 4. Follow the same steps.

I have published the changes in the HelloServer project at http://bonaventuresystems.com/Apress/ BeginningHMAD/CH07/SayHello.ashx.

```csharp
public class SayHello : IHttpHandler
{
    public void ProcessRequest(HttpContext context)
    {
        // Below line is to convey client browser / hybrid application
        // that we are retunring data in JSON format

        context.Response.ContentType = "text/json";

        // Create a person class object's collection
        // Assign dummy information to the same. Consider as if information comes from DB

        Person person1 = new Person() { No = 1, Name = "James", Address = "London" };
        Person person2 = new Person() { No = 2, Name = "Jack", Address = "Newyork" };
        Person person3 = new Person() { No = 3, Name = "Rita", Address = "Boston" };
        Person person4 = new Person() { No = 4, Name = "Celestin", Address = "SF" };

        List<Person> people = new List<Person>() { person1, person2, person3, person4 };

        string jsonResult = string.Empty;

        // Create Javascript serializer helper object
        // Need to refer below namespace for the same
        // Put using "System.Web.Script.Serialization"

        JavaScriptSerializer jss = new JavaScriptSerializer();

        // Serialize person's data in JSON format
        jsonResult = jss.Serialize(people);

        // Write JSON data to browser / App
        context.Response.Write(jsonResult);
        context.Response.AppendHeader("Access-Control-Allow-Origin", "*");
    }

    public bool IsReusable
    {
        get
        {
            return false;
        }
    }
}
```

Figure 7-1. *Changes in SayHello.ashx*

After deployment, Figure 7-2 is the direct JSON output shown on the Chrome browser UI.

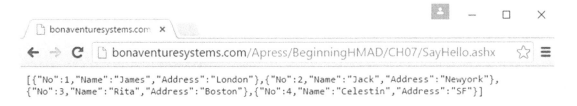

[{"No":1,"Name":"James","Address":"London"},{"No":2,"Name":"Jack","Address":"Newyork"},
{"No":3,"Name":"Rita","Address":"Boston"},{"No":4,"Name":"Celestin","Address":"SF"}]

Figure 7-2. JSON output from SayHello.ashx

So, testing through the browser is done for SayHello.ashx.
Now, let's focus on the client side.

1. Open the HelloClient project used in Chapter 4.

2. Open index.html. Figure 7-3 explains the changes to be made in index.html, along with comments.

```html
<html>
<head>
    <title>Say Hi</title>
    <script src="jquery-1.11.3.min.js"></script>
    <link rel="stylesheet" href="bootstrap.min.css" />
    <script src="bootstrap.min.js"></script>
    <script>
        $(document).ready(function () {
            $('#btnCallServer').click(function () {
                $.ajax({
                    url: 'http://bonaventuresystems.com/Apress/BeginningHMAD/CH07/SayHello.ashx',
                    type: 'GET',
                    success: function (result)
                    {
                        var template1 = '<div class="col-lg-3">Name: <input type="text" id="txtName" value="';
                        var template2 = '<div class="col-lg-3">Address: <input type="text" id="txtAddress" value="';
                        var template3 = '<div class="col-lg-3"><input type="button" id="btnSayHi" value="Say Hi" /></div>';
                        var template4 = '" /></div>';
                        var oneRecord = '' ;
                        for (var i = 0; i < result.length; i++) {
                            oneRecord = oneRecord + template1 + result[i].Name + template4 + template2 + result[i].Address + template4 + template3;
                        }
                        $('#container').append(oneRecord);
                    },
                    error: function (err)
                    {
                        debugger;
                        alert('Error!');
                    }
                });
            });
        });
    </script>
</head>
<body>
    <input type="button" id="btnCallServer" value="Call Server" />
    <br /><br /><br />
    <div class="container" id="container">
    </div>
</body>
</html>
```

Changed URL

Creating UI dynamically based on data available

Changes in the body code. Only div with id "container" exists

Figure 7-3. Client-side changes in index.html

3. Once done with the changes described in Figure 7-3, you can test index.html in the browser.

4. Run it and then click Call Server. The click-event raises a call to the server-side SayHello.ashx.

View the data that appears in the dynamically constructed UI. After viewing it, try to resize the browser to "literally" mobile size. Note that the change in the UI is due to classes added in templates 1, 2, and 3 as col-lg-3. Figure 7-4 shows the dynamic UI appearance when viewed on a mobile-size screen.

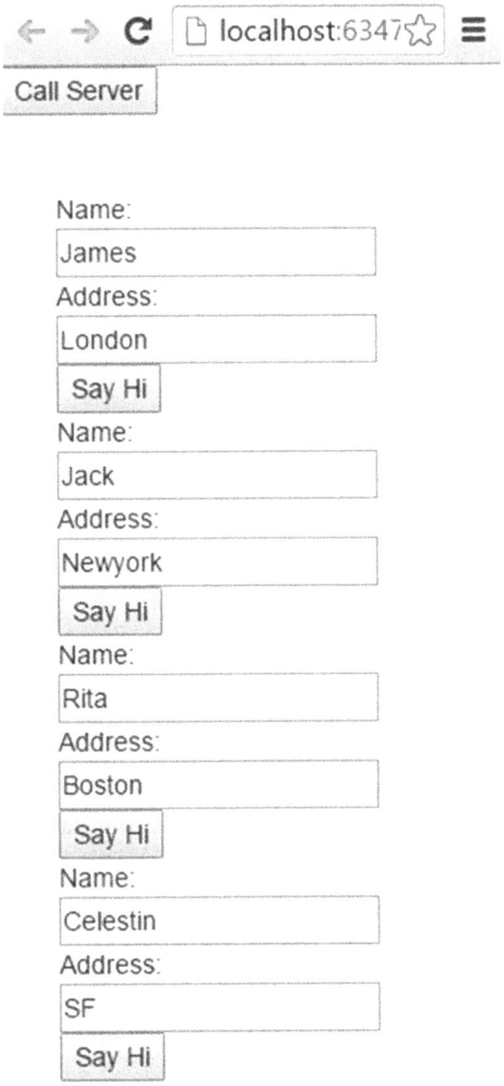

Figure 7-4. *Dynamic UI building*

133

Event Handling in JQuery

Notice that the Say Hi button is replicated in each record sent by the server. As of now, there is no code to handle the Say Hi button click event. Suppose that you write a function in JavaScript named F1 (). How do you tell each Say Hi button to execute F1 ()? Moreover, how will F1 () will identify which button was clicked?

Let's solve these problems one by one.

Live Event Binding in JQuery Using On ()

First problem: Tell each dynamically added button which function to execute. Solution: Let's use an on () function in JQuery. It works only with JQuery 1.7 and above.

As per the JQuery web site (http://api.jquery.com/on/), the on () function attaches an event handler function of one or more events to the selected elements. The live () functionality was used in JQuery until version 1.9. Today, the on () function's performance is considered better than live ().

Add the snippet shown in Figure 7-5 after the first line of JavaScript code (i.e., after "$(document).ready (function () {").

```
$(document).on("click", "#btnSayHi", function () {
    alert('hi!');
});
```

Figure 7-5. *JQuery on ( ) functionality code*

Run the page again and make sure that on the click of any Say Hi button, an alert dialog with a "Hi" message appears.

Why can't you use the normal click () function in JQuery, which you used for the Call Server button? Use the click () function, which helps attach a click event of the controls with the respective event handler function. This works provided control exists in the Document Object Model (DOM) tree at the time the tree is created; this means that control is statically hard-coded into the HTML design.

In scenario discussed earlier, the Say Hi buttons are added to the DOM tree at runtime based on data received from the server. So, to register dynamically added controls plus their events in the DOM tree, use the on () function. Another function, bind () in JQuery 1.9+ only uses on () internally.

Now, only "Hi" is printed in the dialog box. We want a person's name appended to "Hi".

Second problem: How to keep a track of which Say Hi button is clicked? Solution: Use JQuery to find information about the current button or control being clicked, which is done using "$(this)". But since every button added in the UI has same id, name, and attribute, it becomes very difficult to identify the control. So, why not add an extra attribute with a record-specific value while constructing the button programmatically? Let's add a "Name of person" value to title attribute of the button. Note these changes in Figure 7-6.

```
$(document).on("click", "#btnSayHi", function () {
    var nameData = $(this).attr('title');
    alert('hi! ' + nameData);
});
```

$(this) means current "btnSayHi" being clicked.
attr('title') means we are asking JQuery to get
'title' attribute value from current button

```
success: function (result)
{
    var template1 = '<div class="col-lg-3">Name: <input type="text" id="txtName" value="';
    var template2 = '<div class="col-lg-3">Address: <input type="text" id="txtAddress" value="';
    var template3 = '<div class="col-lg-3"><input type="button" id="btnSayHi" value="Say Hi" title="';
    var template4 = '" /></div>';
    var oneRecord = '' ;
    for (var i = 0; i < result.length; i++) {
        oneRecord = oneRecord + template1 + result[i].Name + template4 + template2 + result[i].Address +
                    template4 + template3 + result[i].Name + template4;

    }
    $('#container').append(oneRecord);
},
```

Appending "Name" of the person as an titile
attribute value; which will fetched later

Figure 7-6. *Dynamic UI generation along with use of on() function*

Now you see an alert dialog showing "hi!" and a person's name appended, as shown in Figure 7-7.

Figure 7-7. *Dynamic UI in browser*

JQuery Plug-in-based Approach to Generating a UI

Notice in the code that the entire dynamic UI generation is based on the for loop. Instead of using the for loop, can we define the <TEMPLATE> based approach? What is it? And what can this approach do? It means that instead of using template 1,2,3,4 and the "append only" approach, we define the entire person-related reusable UI along with the data holder. This approach helps reduce memory utilization.

To achieve this, many JQuery plug-ins (code libraries) exist. Some are paid and some are free. Let's use a free library to generate the UI using s template concept called jsrender.js and available on GitHub (https://github.com/borismoore/jsrender) (see Figure 7-8).

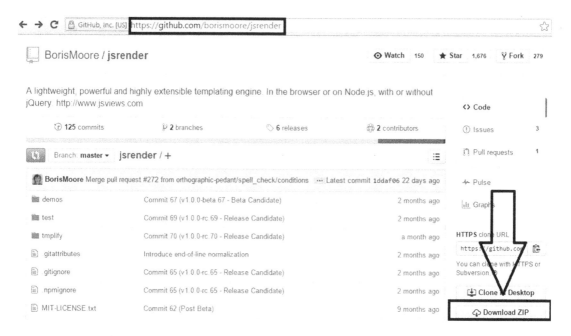

Figure 7-8. *Downloading jsrender.js library*

render.js

1. After downloading compressed (ZIP) content from github.com, uncompress it.

2. Refer jsrender.min.js into index.html.

3. Add a reusable HTML template with content placeholders for the record data. Make changes to the success function, which are shown in Figure 7-9.

```
<script src="jsrender.min.js"></script>

<script type="text/html" id="template">
                              Note template's type is "text/html"
    <div class="col-lg-3">Name: <input type="text" id="txtName" value="{{:Name}}"></div>
    <div class="col-lg-3">Address: <input type="text" id="txtAddress" value="{{:Address}}"></div>
    <div class="col-lg-3"><input type="button" id="btnSayHi" value="Say Hi" title="{{:Name}}"></div>
</script>
```

```
success: function (result)
{
    var allDivs = $('#template').render(result);    //This function is from jsrender.js
    $('#container').append(allDivs);
},
```

Figure 7-9. *Using jsrender.js*

4. Run index.html in a browser. Observe that there is less code but that it still works
    the same as before. Also, note that there is no for loop in the success function.

Miscellaneous Libraries and Plugins

While working with hybrid mobile applications, sometimes you don't have to reinvent the wheel. Simply
find it and use it!

Many developers, companies have already authored plug-ins based on top of Java script or JQuery.
These plug-ins are available for manipulating UI, creating UI effects or for creating dashboards or charts
and so on. Some of the plug-ins are listed next along with short descriptions. The following information may
change from Vendor and is subject to change.

Fusion Chart

A fusion chart is a JavaScript-based charting control library that works on the Web and mobile. It can be
downloaded at http://www.fusioncharts.com. It is available for free or for pay (license cost $199 to $3299).
The following is its list of features:

- Drill-down chart
- Zoom in/out
- Export
- Real time
- Multilingual

Touch Punch

Touch Punch is similar to famous JQUERY UI Library but specifically made to support touch gestures! Download it at `http://touchpunch.furf.com` for free. Its features include drag-and-drop, resize, dialog, slider, and accordion, among available major UI effects. However, to use this library, you have to refer to the JQuery UI library because Touch Punch depends on the JQuery UI.

Responsive UI

You have come across the term *responsive UI* many times since the first chapter. A responsive UI means UI that changes as per the available media device.

If you develop such a UI, you have to measure the available container size and then accordingly set the content size. The efforts required for creating a responsive UI directly depends on how complex the internal UI components and controls are. Instead of reinventing the responsive UI libraries, there are already many available.

The following describes two of the more popular responsive UI libraries or CSS frameworks. The following information may change by vendor and is subject to change.

- Twitter Bootstrap

    - Download at `http://getbootstrap.com/`

    - Paid or Free: Free (MIT License)

    - Features:

        - Developed at Twitter

        - Divides device's screen area (real estate) into a 12-column grid

        - Works on well-known mobile browsers and webviews

- Skeleton

    - Download at `http://getskeleton.com`

    - Paid or Free: Open source MIT license

    - Features:

        - Lightweight

        - Divides device's screen area (real estate) into a 12-column grid

        - Works on most mobile browsers

Frequently Used Style Classes in Bootstrap

To create a complex UI in a hybrid application, you have to understand the style classes available from a responsive UI framework. The following are the bootstrap classes frequently used in hybrid applications and the Web.

- `Table`: Represents a table with prespecified border.

- `table-responsive`: Makes a table responsive.

- `form-control`: Makes any UI HTML control responsive.

- `table-stripped border`: Defines a table with alternate background rows.

- `visible-md`, `visible-sm`, `visible-lg`, and `visible-x`: Defines whether the control is officially visible and the default size (`md` means medium; `sm` means small; `lg` means large; x means extra-small).

- `Nav`: Defines navigation. (LI, UL) needs to be used along with Nav.

- `Span 1 till 12`: For example, if an element size is 12, this means the entire row is occupied by a control if it is a 12-column grid.

Now let's summarize what we have covered in this chapter.

Summary

This chapter covered dynamic UI generation using code. It also discussed the render.js plug-in based on top of JQuery and used to replace the `for` each loop in the UI generation code.

We covered the event handling mechanism using JQuery, specifically live event binding. Finally, we discussed popular plug-ins available on the market related to UI only and responsive UI.

The next chapter discusses how to access device-specific features in hybrid mobile application through code.

CHAPTER 8

■ ■ ■

Using Device Features in HMAD

The objectives of this chapter are to

- Learn how to use device features

- Work with an SD card

- Use camera through plug-ins

- Use the HTML5 Geolocation service

- Learn to create, sync, and update applications

Devices come in various sizes, with various features, and at various prices. This chapter deals with some common device features. Let's start with tracking a geolocation.

Geolocation Services

Many mobile applications (which may or may not be hybrid) can track the location of the user; popular examples include Zomato, Foursquare, and Uber. Applications like Zomato use location as a major input.

Hybrid applications can use the HTML5 Geolocation API. This API uses browser-vendor-specific services to get the user's current latitude, longitude, and altitude. Alternatively, they can use plug-ins to do the same thing.

What are we planning to use in this chapter? Well, Cordova offers an implementation that uses this HTML5-based API at http://docs.telerik.com. We will use the core HTML5 Geolocation API with the navigator DOM object.

Using the HTML5 API

Again, HTML5 offers the Geolocation API with the navigator object. So we will set up index.html (like we used in Chapter 4 with the Telerik AppBuilder). Let's create the following UI along with the DIV container to hold all the data and buttons to call the Navigator API. An explanation of the UI along with the markup is given in Figure 8-1.

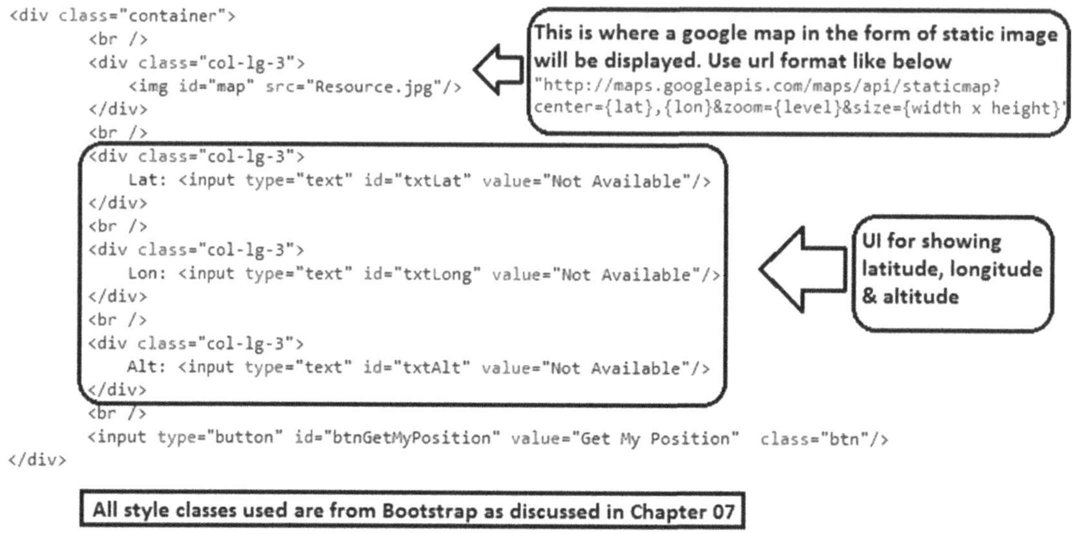

```
<div class="container">
        <br />
        <div class="col-lg-3">
            <img id="map" src="Resource.jpg"/>
        </div>
        <br />
        <div class="col-lg-3">
            Lat: <input type="text" id="txtLat" value="Not Available"/>
        </div>
        <br />
        <div class="col-lg-3">
            Lon: <input type="text" id="txtLong" value="Not Available"/>
        </div>
        <br />
        <div class="col-lg-3">
            Alt: <input type="text" id="txtAlt" value="Not Available"/>
        </div>
        <br />
        <input type="button" id="btnGetMyPosition" value="Get My Position"  class="btn"/>
</div>
```

> This is where a google map in the form of static image will be displayed. Use url format like below
> "http://maps.googleapis.com/maps/api/staticmap?
> center={lat},{lon}&zoom={level}&size={width x height}"

> UI for showing latitude, longitude & altitude

All style classes used are from Bootstrap as discussed in Chapter 07

Figure 8-1. *Responsive UI and styles*

Now, let's add a JavaScript and JQuery code snippet in `index.html`. The JavaScript code explanation is shown in Figure 8-2.

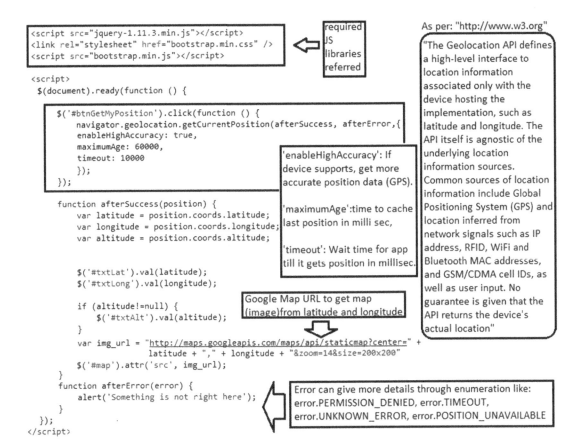

Figure 8-2. *Using the Geolocation API*

As mentioned in the Figure 8-2, you to refer the required JS libraries into the code. On handling the button click, use a callback mechanism. As seen in the code, GetCurrentPosition() expects the first two parameters as callback functions. The first function is called after a successful reply from the server and another is called if any problem or error persists.

The third parameter is a JSON object. It has three keys: enableHighAccuracy, maximumAge, and timeout. All is explained in Figure 8-2. Note that over the Web, the timeout counter starts only after the user permits the application to track his location. Since location is very private user information, the app asks permission before usage or installation.

Along with latitude, longitude, and altitude values, you can also get speed, the time of the server's response, and the direction that user is headed, which is provided in the angle (degrees) format, clockwise from the north.

You can package the preceding code using AppBuilder and run the application, just as we did in Chapter 4.

Geolocation Plug-ins and Helpers

You may use geolocation libraries like GEO.js, which you can download from `https://code.google.com/p/geo-location-javascript`. You can also use the wrapped up HTML5 Geolocation API from Cordova. Sample code is offered on the Telerik AppBuilder web site at `http://docs.telerik.com/platform/samples/sample-geolocation/`.

If you notice, instead of only showing latitude and longitude as numbers, we have used the Google Map API. You can also use third-party APIs to graphically show the location. Microsoft's Bing Maps API is also helpful and easy to use in this case. Follow these steps to use the Microsoft Bing Maps API:

1. Visit `https://www.bingmapsportal.com`.

2. Log in with Live credentials.

3. The user interface will look like the one shown in Figure 8-3.

Figure 8-3. *Creating a key for Bing Maps usage*

4. Click My account ➤ create a new key *or* view/download complete list of keys (see Figure 8-4).

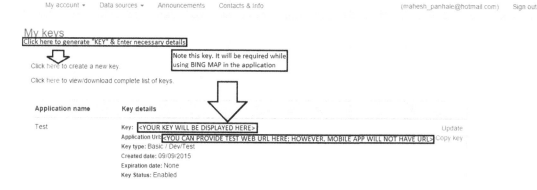

Figure 8-4. *Keys under user's profile*

5. Change the code inside `index.html` (refer to AppBuilder) to the one shown and explained in Figure 8-5.

```
<script charset="UTF-8" type="text/javascript"
  src="http://ecn.dev.virtualearth.net/mapcontrol/mapcontrol.ashx?v=7.0">
</script>
```
Script required for Microsoft.Maps.Map object

```
<script type="text/javascript">

    function CallNavigator() {
        navigator.geolocation.getCurrentPosition(success, error);
    }
```
Same navigator object called in last example

```
    function success(position) {
        var lat = position.coords.latitude;
        var long = position.coords.longitude;

        var coords = new Microsoft.Maps.Map(document.getElementById("mapContainer"),
        { credentials: "Aovbxy6u3U43EVi8G-OQhsI_BhfVL5Xuo8N71qohEsVyC4FdWsn3sovYb_cSXwOn" });

        var location = new Microsoft.Maps.Location(lat, long);
        coords.setView({ zoom: 18. center: location });

        var pin = new Microsoft.Maps.Pushpin(location);
        coords.entities.push(pin);
    }
```
Key passed. Created using https://www.bingmapsportal.com

Bubble to highlight "location"

```
    function error(err) {
        alert('Something is not right here!');
    }

    </script>
</head>
```

```
<body onload="CallNavigator()">
    <div id="mapContainer"></div>
</body>
```
UI for showing "BING" Map at start of the APP itself

Figure 8-5. *Using Microsoft Bing Maps API for geolocation*

6. After the build, deploy the code as in Chapter 4.

So, you can refer HTML5 or third-party plug-ins to show the geolocation of a user. The workings of the HTML5 Geolocation API are complex because it works against device-specific algorithms. It is dependent on the availability of an Internet connection, GPS, and so on.

Now, let's focus on SD cards.

I/O Operations

Some applications do not require Internet connectivity. To maintain the user's data, such an application may use an SD card (a small flash memory card designed to for higher storage) or phone internal storage.

Offline applications may use an SD card or the phone's internal storage. Applications such as WhatsApp may use an SD card or the phone's internal storage to store data received from the Internet. This is a feature that cannot be tested on a simulator. It has to be tested on a real device.

An application that requires access to the user's SD card or internal phone storage has to get permission from the user during installation.

When working with hybrid applications, there are many APIs available for an SD card or internal phone storage, including the READ/ WRITE operation. You can also use core the HTML5 file I/O access feature as well. More information about HTML5's file access feature is available at http://www.w3.org/TR/FileAPI/.

Let's use a core HTML5-based API to work with an SD card or internal phone storage. You have to refer to a window object from the DOM tree to work with memory.

Let's make step-by-step changes to the application.

1. Open index.html from the existing project (see Chapter 4).

2. Make changes in the markup as per Figure 8-6. Keep a note that the app. initialize() method is referred to handle the device initialization event. The code for this function is authored in the index.js file.

```html
<div class="container">

    <div class="col-lg-3">
        Name: <input type="text" id="txtName" value="" />
    </div>
    <div class="col-lg-3">
        Address: <input type="text" id="txtAddress" value="" />
    </div>
    <div class="col-lg-3">
        <input type="button" id="btnStore" value="Write to SD Card" />
    </div>
    <div class="col-lg-3">
        <input type="button" id="btnFetch" value="Read from Card" />
    </div>
     <div id="deviceready" class="blink">
            <p class="event listening">Connecting to Device</p>
            <p class="event received">Device is Ready</p>
     </div>
  <script type="text/javascript" src="cordova.js"></script>
    <script type="text/javascript" src="index.js"></script>
  <script type="text/javascript">
        app.initialize();
  </script>
</div>
```

[Annotation: UI for Read, Write operations on mobile drive]

Figure 8-6. *UI for Read/Write on mobile device*

3. Now, after <body> tag–related changes, add the following JavaScript code into index.html. The code mentioned in Figure 8-7 is self-explanatory.

```
<script>
    $(document).ready(function () {
        var fileSystem = null;
        $('#btnStore').click(function () {
            window.requestFileSystem(LocalFileSystem.PERSISTENT, 0, afterSuccess, afterError);
        });
        function afterSuccess(fs) {
            fileSystem = fs;
            fileSystem.root.getFile( 'apress.json' , { create: true }, afterFileCreate);
        }
                        can be other file as well
        function afterFileCreate(currentFile) {
            currentFile.createWriter(afterWriterCreated);
        }

        function afterWriterCreated(writer) {
            var jsonData = { Name: $('#txtName').val(), Address: $('#txtAddress').val() };
            writer.write(JSON.stringify(jsonData));
        }                            Final write on filesystem

        function afterError(error) {
            alert('something wrong!');
        }

        $('#btnFetch').click(function () {
            var filePath = fileSystem.root.toURL() + "/" + "apress.json";
            alert(filePath);
            $.ajax({         file:///storage/emulated/0//apress.json
                url: filePath,
                success: function (jsonData) {
                    alert(jsonData);
                },
                error: function (err) { alert('something wrong!');}
            });
        });
    });
</script>
```

LocalFileSystem can be:

Persistent: User's permission is required while deleting

Temporary: Browser can take adhocdecision based on memory available

using "ajax" is not mandatory. One may use traditional HTML 5 base code like:
fileSystem.root.getFile('apress.json', {create:false},callbackFn);

Figure 8-7. File I/O code

4. Don't forget to add a reference to the required JS libraries, as mentioned in Figure 8-8.

```
<script src="jquery-1.11.3.min.js"></script>
<link rel="stylesheet" href="bootstrap.min.css" />
<script src="bootstrap.min.js"></script>
```
Reference files required for UI and JQuery

Figure 8-8. References into the code

5. Make sure that you also refer the index.js file code at the root of the application. Replace code, if any, from index.js, as shown in Figure 8-9.

```
var app = {
    // Application Constructor
    initialize: function() {
        this.bindEvents();
    },
    // Bind Event Listeners
    //
    // Bind any events that are required on startup. Common events are:
    // 'load', 'deviceready', 'offline', and 'online'.
    bindEvents: function() {
        document.addEventListener('deviceready', this.onDeviceReady, false);
    },
    // deviceready Event Handler
    //
    // The scope of 'this' is the event. In order to call the 'receivedEvent'
    // function, we must explicity call 'app.receivedEvent(...);'

    onDeviceReady: function() {
        app.receivedEvent('deviceready');
        navigator.splashscreen.hide();

    },
    // Update DOM on a Received Event
    receivedEvent: function(id) {
        var parentElement = document.getElementById(id);
        var listeningElement = parentElement.querySelector('.listening');
        var receivedElement = parentElement.querySelector('.received');

        listeningElement.setAttribute('style', 'display:none;');
        receivedElement.setAttribute('style', 'display:block;');

        console.log('Received Event: ' + id);
    }
};
```

Callout (top): Handles default event related to "device ready"

Figure 8-9. *Handling device-ready event*

6. After this, compile and build the code. Keep in mind that since it involves interaction with the device, this app cannot be tested with an online simulator.

7. Build it for Android, deploy it, and test it.

8. After deployment (I did the test on Samsung Note 2), the app UI looks like what's shown in Figure 8-10.

Figure 8-10. *UI after running code on Android device*

9. Make an entry in the Name and the Address fields. Click Write to SD Card
   (see Figure 8-11).

Figure 8-11. *Writing content on device*

10. The file is saved on the file system's root. Now, click Read from Card. If you have
    noticed, we have used the AJAX function to read the data from the drive. But the
    URL parameter in JQuery AJAX requires URLs with a pattern. So, to access the file
    on the file system, you can use the native URL functionality offered by the plug-in.

11. Figure 8-12 shows the alert, which in turn shows the native file system URL to access the file.

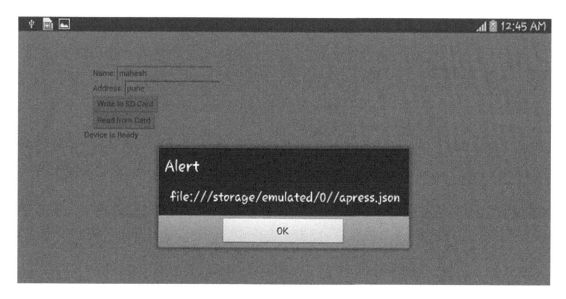

Figure 8-12. *Native file system–based URL for the JSON file*

The final alert dialog appears (see Figure 8-13) along with data in the form of string, which can be JSON parsed later. The file created on the file system can be seen by navigating through My Files, as shown in Figure 8-14.

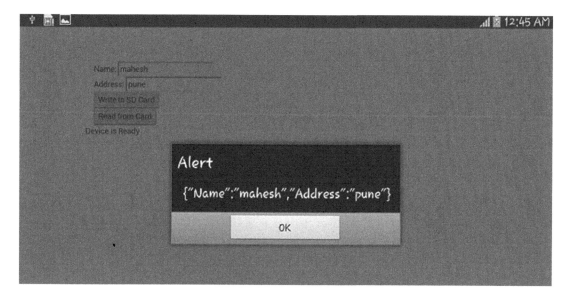

Figure 8-13. *JSON file contents*

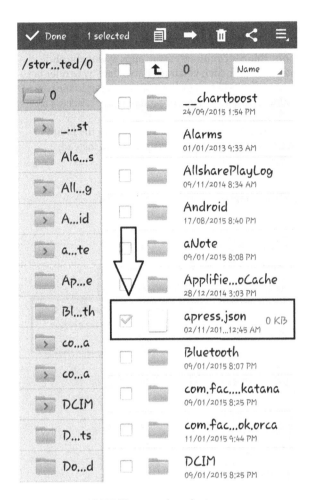

Figure 8-14. *JSON file created on device*

Along with the preceding basic functionality, you can also use the following functions available from the LocalFileSystem API:

- getDirectory(): Get folders inside the file system. You can create a folder with {Create: true} as the JSON parameter.

- readEntries(): A function available with the Reader. It helps read files available based on the directory. It offers collection as output, but in a callback way.

- moveTo(): As the name suggests, this function helps move files from one folder to another.

- copyTo(): As the name suggests, this function helps copy files from one folder to another.

Now, let's focus on working with camera, which is one of the most popular features.

Access and Use a Device-Based Camera

Whether it's WhatsApp, Facebook, Twitter, or so forth, one thing is commonly seen: apps asking the end user for profile photos. If a photo is not available on the file system, then you must have a facility to offer to the end user that allows him or her to use the device's camera to take a snapshot. This is similar to the way shoot-and-share applications like Instagram demand a lot of camera usage. So, camera usage is necessary nowadays.

Using HTML5 and JavaScript, you can again use the navigator DOM object to get most of the photo work done. How do you work with a camera? We won't be working with any external plug-in; instead, geolocation and file I/O, we will use only HTML5-specific code.

Let's learn how to access a camera, step by step:

1. Open index.html from the existing project (see Chapter 4).

2. Make changes in the markup, as per Figure 8-15.

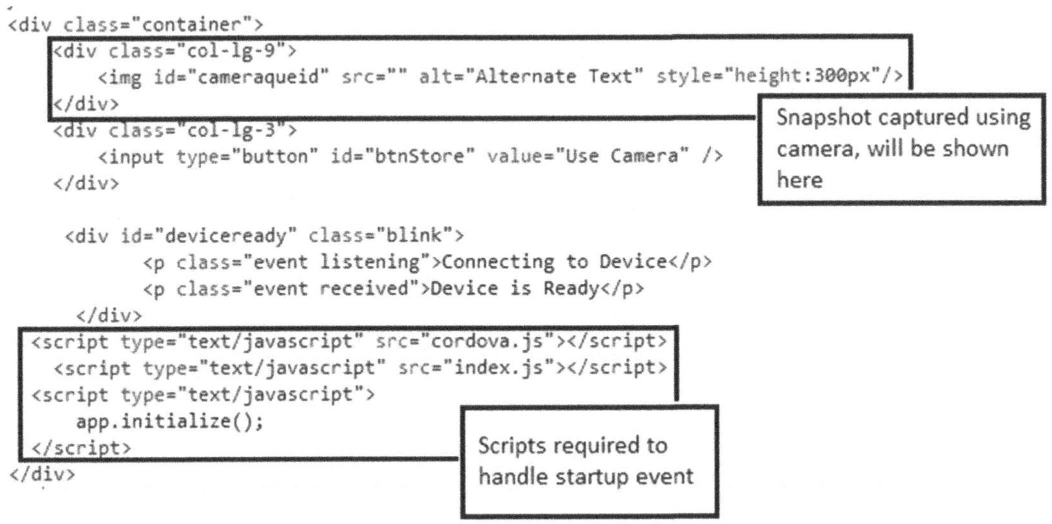

```
<div class="container">
    <div class="col-lg-9">
        <img id="cameraqueid" src="" alt="Alternate Text" style="height:300px"/>
    </div>
    <div class="col-lg-3">
        <input type="button" id="btnStore" value="Use Camera" />
    </div>

    <div id="deviceready" class="blink">
            <p class="event listening">Connecting to Device</p>
            <p class="event received">Device is Ready</p>
    </div>
<script type="text/javascript" src="cordova.js"></script>
    <script type="text/javascript" src="index.js"></script>
<script type="text/javascript">
    app.initialize();
</script>
</div>
```

Snapshot captured using camera, will be shown here

Scripts required to handle startup event

Figure 8-15. *UI for camera capture*

3. Make sure you refer to the required JS libraries, such as Bootstrap and JQuery.

4. Add the JS code from Figure 8-16. Note the explanation of the code.

```
<script>

    $(document).ready(function () {

            $('#btnStore').click(function () {

                navigator.camera.getPicture(OnSuccess, onFailure,
                    {
                        quality: 50,
                        destinationType : Camera.DestinationType.DATA_URL,
                        sourceType : Camera.PictureSourceType.CAMERA,
                        encodingType: Camera.EncodingType.JPEG,
                        targetWidth: 500,
                        targetHeight: 500,
                        correctOrientation: true,
                        saveToPhotoAlbum: false
                    });
            });
        function OnSuccess(imageData) {
            alert('Success');
            var smallImage = document.getElementById("cameraqueid");
            smallImage.style.display = 'block';
            smallImage.src = "data:image/jpeg;base64," + imageData;
            alert('Done');
        }

        function onFailure(err) {
            alert('Something wrong!');
        }

    });

</script>
```

Important Parameters:
1) quality: It means quality of image. Valid values are 0 to 100
2) destinationType: It means data format. Valid values are:
        DATA_URL: base64 string
        FILE_URI: fileURI
3) sourceType: Camera or photo library
4) encodingType: JPEG or PNG

Figure 8-16. *Using camera features*

5. Compile and build the code. Keep in mind that since it involves interaction with the device, this app cannot be tested with an online simulator.

6. So, build it for Android, deploy it, and test it.

7. After deployment (I did the test on Samsung Note 2), the app UI should look like what's shown in Figure 8-17.

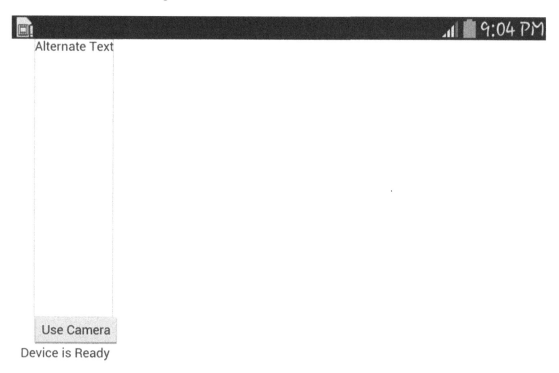

Figure 8-17. *UI for Camera Capture Code*

8. Click Use Camera to start the camera. Take a snapshot. I took a picture of a company logo. After accepting the snapshot, it is displayed, as shown in Figure 8-18.

Figure 8-18. *Camera being accessed*

Access a Unique ID

There will be times that you want to find a unique identifier for the device using your hybrid application. The purpose could be for identifying who used the application. You can access a device unique identifier with the help of device.uuid (see Figure 8-19). You may want to know a device unique ID regardless of the phone or SIM number; for example, an offline application in Domain Survey. (Domain Survey is explained in the Case Study, later in the book.)

```
use "device.uuid" to get unique ID of device on which your
hybrid application is running
```

Figure 8-21. *Getting unique ID of the device*

Building Offline Applications

Sometimes Internet connectivity is not available but applications have to continue working. In such situations, can applications continue storing data and keep running as offline applications? Yes. To check Internet availability, you can use the connection object, exposed via the navigator.connection.

However, if you keep the availability check against a timer in JS, then that may lead to higher battery usage, in which case your application could get banned from a mobile vendor store! To check the battery status (to take some ad hoc action) through code, refer to Figure 8-20.

```
window.addEventListener("batterystatus", onBatteryStatus, false)
                                          works on callback!
```

Figure 8-20. *Using offline APIs*

To store data locally on the file system, we have already seen the Storage approach. You can also use HTML5's Window.localStorage to store key-value pair-based data.

To sync such data with the server on the network, you may use AJAX with an HTTP handler, web service, or WCF service on the server side.

Common Issues and Solutions

One common problem of working with these features is the user interface. Since the code for hybrid application works inside the webview (internally, webview works with a similar default browser engine), rendering the engine may rarely create a problem.

At the same time, when it comes to Apple UI standards, you have to pay good attention to it. As discussed, if the application uses the device's battery to a great extent, then the greater the chance that the application will not get approval on a vendor's mobile store. Since most of the UI code is done in the index. html file, maintenance can become a problem.

Patterns and Practices

It is always recommended that if you have even the smallest clue that your application's code size will grow, then you should use an MV*-like pattern in the client-side code of the application from the onset of the project. That means use the MV* framework in HTML JavaScript code.

One such framework that has gained popularity recently is AngularJS.

Tips and Tricks

It is recommended that while working with LOCALSTORAGE, test the functionality with the browser first and then build it against mobile. Similarly, if targeting geolocation, use simulators to test the application. Use actual test devices while working with the camera, SD cards, and sensor-like features.

Let's summarize what we have learned.

Summary

This chapter discussed accessing device features, such as geolocation tracking, the camera, and the file system. With these features, we stuck to core HTML5-specific code rather than third-party plug-ins.

Considering only the features covered in this chapter, the major issues of deploying applications exist because of UI load time and battery consumption. These are norms that you must understand when creating UI-centric applications for specific mobile devices.

The next chapter discusses third-party code and library integration in hybrid mobile applications.

■ ■ ■

How to Advertise with HMAD

The objectives of this chapter are to

- Understand why to use advertisements

- Learn about earning through advertisements

- Learn the different advertisement frameworks

- Learn how to set up and use AdMob account

- Understand the guidelines

This chapter is interesting because it deals with money-earning techniques. Do you regularly purchase mobile apps from an app store? Many of us are always looking for free apps. Specifically, Android lacks good applications available for free.

What's in it for a developer or a company that creates free applications? How do they earn money? Is advertisement money sufficient to drive a big company or an individual?

Well, again, we have the consultant's answer for all questions. It depends. It depends on many factors: How good is your app? How do you market your app? How big is the audience for your app?

Let's take one crazy example of earning through ads. Have you heard of a game called Flappy Bird (https://en.wikipedia.org/wiki/Flappy_Bird)?

Flappy Bird is a game developed by Vietnam-based developer Dong Nguyen. In this game, the player tries to control a bird flying through rows of bars/pipes. The goal is to help the bird fly through obstacles. This game was developed with advertisements as a source of income. The game gained insane popularity in the iStore. Per Wikipedia, the developer claims to earn $50,000 per day.

The point of this example is that if the work is quality and if the application can reach a maximum audience, then the sky is the limit for earning through ads.

Current Market Trends

If you have knowledge about the Web, specifically HTML and JavaScript, then you can develop hybrid applications targeting well-known platforms.

The current market trend is in Android. Mobiles based on Android are available at a low cost. The advertisement business mostly works in volume. Whether it's android, iPhone, or Windows—free is always preferred over paid. How do you offer quality work for free? The solution lies in ads!

Currently, even individual software vendors and freelancers prefer to develop applications for well-known platforms—with only a PC, an Internet connection, and an app store account as investments.

Ad Frameworks

Wait, did I mention fees for advertisement providers? No, but most of the well-known ad providers do provide services for free.

Many of us have heard of Google AdSense. Google AdSense APIs are for web sites. AdMob APIs are from Google but for mobiles. There are many advertisement solution providers, including PubMatic, Microsoft pubCenter, Apple iAd, InMobi, and more. Now, which one to choose? You may prefer to choose ad providers that pay more.

People prefer assurance. People prefer ad solutions from companies like Google, Microsoft, and Apple because these are the giants in the market. Business also depends on the number of ad vendors the ad solution provider has. If you use X ad service provider, then few or no ads may be available in a specific geographical region. In such cases, if you stick with single advertisement vendor, then you may not have any business because it directly depends on whether the ad solution provider has ads in a specific region.

Could you engage your app with many solution providers at the same time? How would you do this? You can use an ad mediator. With an ad mediator, you can register multiple advertisement solution providers for a single app. You can then decide the percentage of ads to flow from a particular provider; for example: 50% AdMob, 30% PubMatic, 20% iAd.

A monetize dashboard is available with an ad mediator, in which you can check the business made from various providers on a period basis. Based on the report, you can change the percentages to make more business.

Do you get paid while testing the app? The short answer is No. Ad solutions providers can detect simulation programs, but you do not get payment from advertisements shown while testing the app.

It may make anyone crazy if a genuine click on an ad is considered by ad providers as fake, simulated, or deliberate click. To differentiate between a testing app and a production-level app, ad providers ask developers to place a flag that indicates whether the application is in test mode or in release mode. The flag names differ from provider to provider.

Google AdSense (Google AdMob for Mobiles)

AdMob is one a very popular advertisement provider for mobile applications— native as well as hybrid.
According to Google:

- AdMob has paid over $1 billion to developers since July 2012

- Over 200 billion ads are shown globally per month

- More than 1,000,000 advertisement vendors use AdMob

- More than 650,000 apps use AdMob as their ad solution provider

- Payments are processed in the local currency

Let's set up a Google AdMob account to get ads for the hybrid application developed in Chapter 4. If you already have an AdSense account, it can be easily linked with AdMob.

Mobile Ad Frameworks: A Quick Comparison

Many advertisement frameworks can be used by mobile applications. Some of these ad frameworks are compared in Table 9-1. Note that the payment information in Table 9-1 is subject to change by the ad provider. Information about banner ads and interstitial ads is covered later in this chapter.

Table 9-1. *Ad Frameworks*

Points/Framework	AdMob	iAd	pubCenter	InMobi	Flurry
Company	Google	Apple	Microsoft	InMobi	Yahoo!
Ad types	Banner, Interstitial	Banner, Interstitial	Banner (Interstitial was recently added) More: adsinapps. microsoft.com	Banner, Interstitial	Banner
Uniqueness	Easy to set up. Also has a mediator facility	Only for Apple devices	Analytics dashboard	Ads are targeted using appographic approach, which means based on the type of apps installed on a user's mobile device.	Analytics dashboard
Minimum amount completion for payment	$100 (Payments made in local currency)	$150 (Not available for all regions)	$50 (Not available for all regions)	$50 in India, $300 outside India	$100
Payment Cycle(if criteria meets)	21st of every month	Per calendar Fiscal month	Within 30 days	Monthly	45 days from the request

Using the AdMob Framework

Let's create an AdMob id and learn how to include ads in our mobile application. We will also deploy this app on mobile and test it. AdMob was chosen because it is easy to set up. You may evaluate other frameworks and use any of them.

The following are the important steps to note in this procedure:

- App registration

- Injecting an ad plug-in

- Including advertisements in the application

- Testing

- Deployment

To create an AdMob ID, do the following:

1. Visit the AdMob web site at `https://apps.admob.com`.

2. You may be asked to log in with Google credentials or you may be redirected to another URL if already logged in.

3. A signup page appears, as shown in Figure 9-1, at `https://apps.admob.com/admob/signup`.

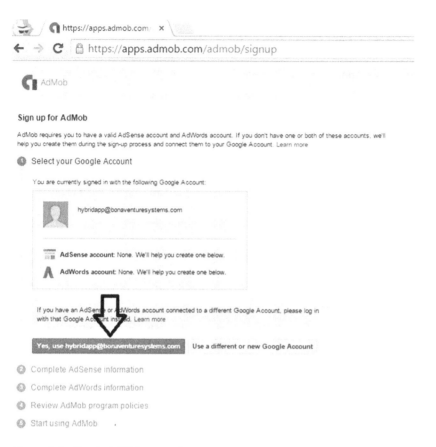

Figure 9-1. *Create AdMob account*

4. The signup screen asks whether to continue with the logged in account or any other account.

5. Click Yes. Use hybridapp@bonaventuresystems.com, as highlighted in Figure 9-1.

6. Next, AdMob asks you to complete profile information to create a Google AdSense account.

7. Complete the information as an individual or business account—whichever is appropriate. I did it as shown in Figure 9-2.

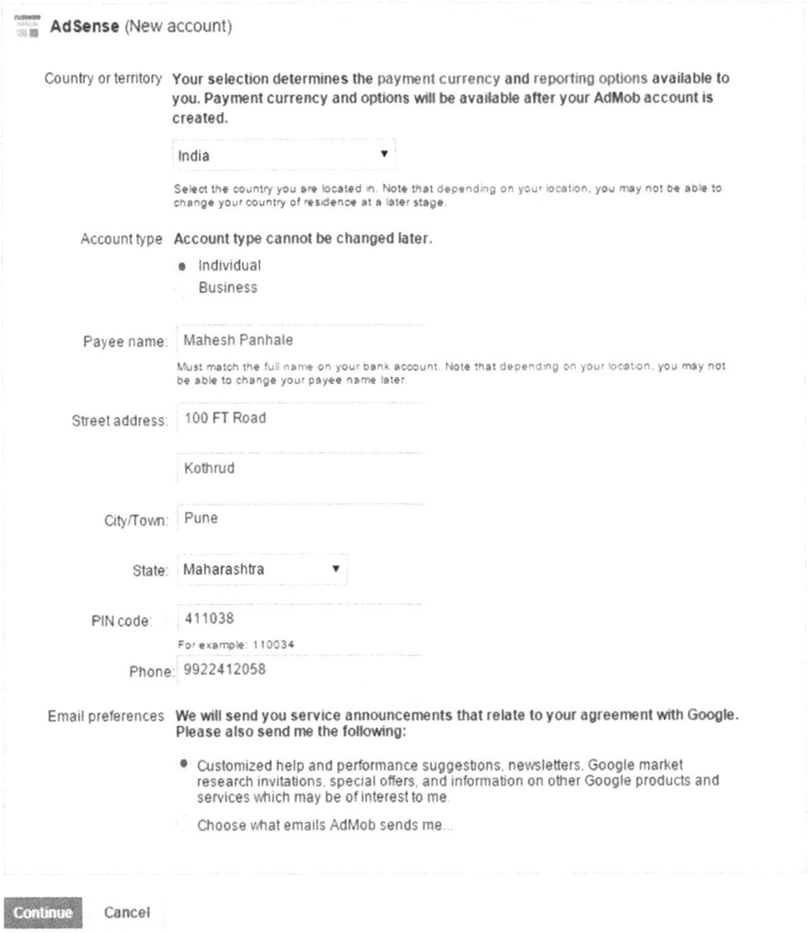

AdSense (New account)

Country or territory   Your selection determines the payment currency and reporting options available to you. Payment currency and options will be available after your AdMob account is created.

India ▼

Select the country you are located in. Note that depending on your location, you may not be able to change your country of residence at a later stage.

Account type   Account type cannot be changed later.
  ● Individual
     Business

Payee name: Mahesh Panhale

Must match the full name on your bank account. Note that depending on your location, you may not be able to change your payee name later.

Street address: 100 FT Road

Kothrud

City/Town: Pune

State: Maharashtra ▼

PIN code: 411038
For example: 110034

Phone: 9922412058

Email preferences   We will send you service announcements that relate to your agreement with Google. Please also send me the following:

  ● Customized help and performance suggestions, newsletters, Google market research invitations, special offers, and information on other Google products and services which may be of interest to me.

     Choose what emails AdMob sends me...

Continue   Cancel

Figure 9-2. *AdMob new user registration process*

8.   Click Continue.

9.   If the account that you logged in with is associated with Google AdWords, then nothing new; otherwise, you have to provide information (like what's shown in Figure 9-3) to create an AdWords account.

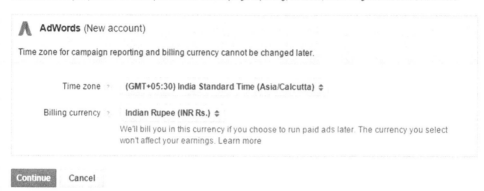

③ Complete AdWords information

Since we couldn't find an existing AdWords account, you'll need to provide some information for AdMob to create one for you. The information you provide will affect your AdMob ad campaign reporting, statistics, and billing information. Learn more

Ⱥ AdWords (New account)

Time zone for campaign reporting and billing currency cannot be changed later.

Time zone ›   (GMT+05:30) India Standard Time (Asia/Calcutta) ⇵

Billing currency ›   Indian Rupee (INR Rs.) ⇵

We'll bill you in this currency if you choose to run paid ads later. The currency you select won't affect your earnings. Learn more

Continue   Cancel

Figure 9-3. AdMob time and currency configuration

10.   Click Continue.

11.   Next, you have to go through AdMob program and policies. After accepting AdMob's program policies, click the Create AdMob account (see Figure 9-4).

④ Review AdMob program policies

☑ I have read and agree to abide by the program policies and Terms & Conditions. I understand that failure to comply with the policies could lead to ads or account being disabled permanently.

You are about to create an AdSense and AdWords account which will be connected to this AdMob account. If you remove yourself from any of these accounts, you will lose access to your AdMob account. Learn more

Create AdMob Account   Cancel

Figure 9-4. AdMob account creation final Step

12.   Click Get Started, as shown in Figure 9-5.

⑤ Start using AdMob

Welcome to AdMob! You are ready to start monetizing and promoting apps.

Get Started

Figure 9-5. AdMob: Getting Started

164

13. You arrive at the home page at `https://apps.admob.com/#home`. Note that there is a publisher id for the account (see Figure 9-6).

Figure 9-6. *AdMob profile home page*

14. Look for the Monetize tab, highlighted in Figure 9-6.

15. Click the Monetize tab. You see an application to use AdMob's advertisements. You can use the search option if the application is already registered with Google Play, iTunes, or the App Store.

16. The test application that we created in Chapter 4 doesn't fit the criteria. So we can use the "Add your app manually" option, highlighted in Figure 9-7.

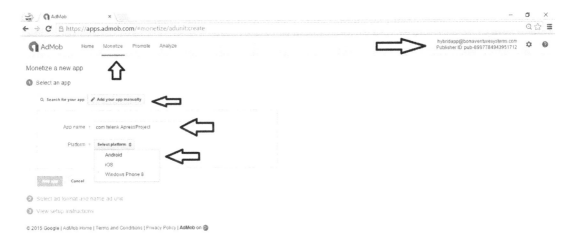

Figure 9-7. *AdMob: Monetize app*

Suggestion: Use the same name for the app that is in the properties panel of Telerik AppBuilder. The application identifier in the properties is also preferred.

Note the following highlighted parts.

- Publisher ID

- Monetize tab

- Add you app manually

- The app name copied from the AppBuilder project (double click the Properties icon inside the Apress Project under Solution Explorer), as shown in Figure 9-8.

Figure 9-8. *Adding AdMob plug-in for mobile application*

17. Now, switch context back to AdMob. After all the information is completed, click Add app.

This action brings up a very interesting screen. Now, you have to choose the ad formats. The two well-known formats are banner and interstitial.

Banner Ads

Banners are small ads that are shown at the bottom or the top of the screen (see Figure 9-9).

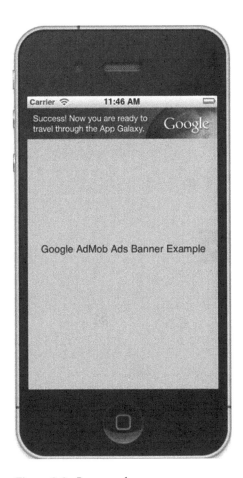

Figure 9-9. *Banner ad*

In the same window, you can configure whether to allow only text-based ads or images, as shown in Figure 9-10.

Figure 9-10. *AdMob: Configure banner ad*

The refresh rate conveys whether to automatically refresh after a certain interval or to not refresh at all. The "Text ad style" option can be customized. You can also choose the color and text displayed in the ad.

Provide an "Ad unit name" as shown in Figure 9-10, because it may help later when there are a greater number of ads configured.

Interstitial

Interstitial ads are shown on a full screen. You can have a choice for ad size and style. You can make a choice which kind of ads should be supported: text, images, or videos.

Offer a value in the "Ad unit name" text box. I entered Apress Test Banner. The final configuration is shown in Figure 9-11.

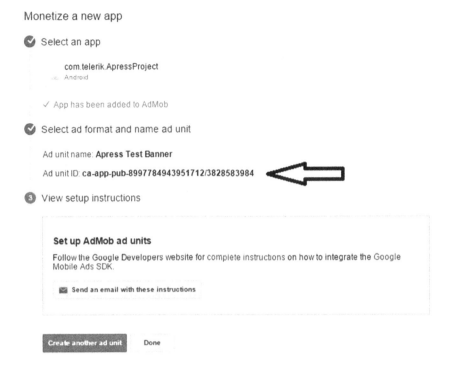

Figure 9-11. *AdMob: Final configuration*

Note that, you can set up many ads this way. Notice the highlighted "Ad unit id" in Figure 9-11, which is the unique identifier. It is used while displaying ads in a hybrid application. For native SDK, there are instructions options that you can receive by email (see Figure 9-11).

This takes us to the final window, where all ad units are shown together in Figure 9-12.

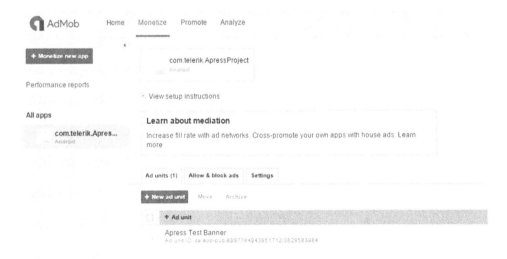

Figure 9-12. *AdMob dashboard*

Make a note of ad unit id, which you'll use to link ads to the app. Meanwhile, after AdWords registration, you receive an e-mail from Google, informing that your account is set up. It also informs you when payment information has changed (see Figure 9-13).

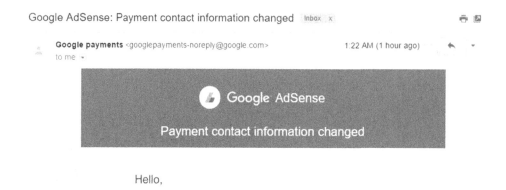

Figure 9-13. *AdMob confirmation e-mail*

You can follow the steps given in the e-mail and complete the information. Keep in mind that account payments are covered in the AdMob's terms and conditions. This is discussed later.

Now let's integrate ads with the project created in Chapter 4.

1. Open `https://platform.telerik.com`. Open Apress Project. The project structure is shown in Figure 9-14.

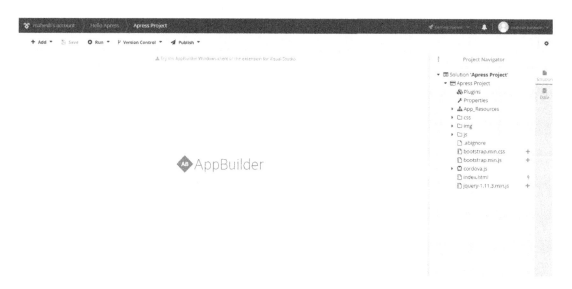

Figure 9-14. *AppBuilder project structure*

2. Double-click Properties ➤ Plug-ins ➤ Install Plugins from Marketplace, as shown in Figure 9-15. (If you don't recall the plug-ins, I recommend reading Chapter 5.)

Figure 9-15. *AppBuilder plug-in addition*

3. In the dialog box, find the AdMob plug-in and click Install (see Figure 9-16).

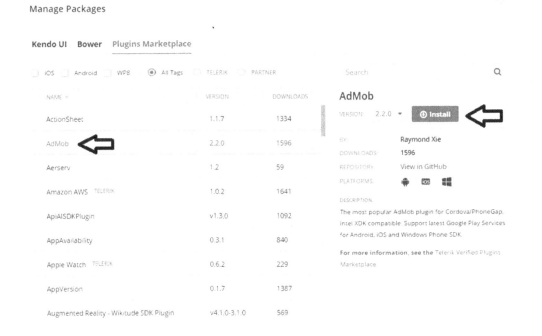

Figure 9-16. *AdMob plug-in installation*

4. After installation, the plug-in is shown in parent windows (see Figure 9-17).

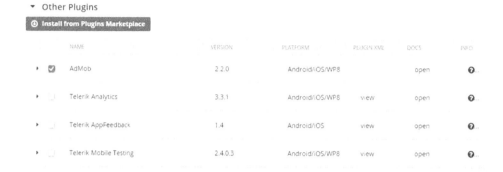

Figure 9-17. AdMob plug-in installation confirmed

5. Go to Project Explorer and find a default file named index.js inside the js folder. Open the file (see Figure 9-18).

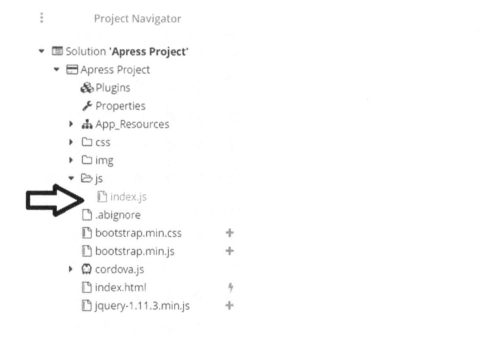

Figure 9-18. AppBuilder project structure

This is the file with the publisher and ad ids generated earlier. There is default code inside this file. Replace the code inside the OnDeviceReady function, as described in Figure 9-19.

```
onDeviceReady: function() {
    app.receivedEvent('deviceready');
    navigator.splashscreen.hide();
        if (window.plugins.AdMob) {
            var admob_key = 'ca-app-pub-8997784943951712/3828583984';
            var am = window.plugins.AdMob;
            am.createBannerView({
                                'publisherId': admob_key,
                                'adSize': am.AD_SIZE.BANNER,
                                'bannerAtTop': true
                    },
                    function() {
                        am.requestAd(
                            { 'isTesting':true },
                            function() {
                                am.showAd(true);
                            },
                            function() {
                                alert('failed to request ad');
                            }
                            );
                    },
                    function() {
                        alert('failed to create banner view');
                    }
                );
        } else {
            alert('AdMob plugin not available/ready.');
        }
},
// Update DOM on a Received Event
```

Figure 9-19. *Integrating AdMob-specific code*

The highlighted code in Figure 9-19 has very important job to do. It mentions the publisher and ad combined value. Before that, we just ensured in the if loop that the plug-in used for advertisements is available and loaded in memory.

bannerAtTop: true denotes that the banner ad will be displayed at the upper side of the screen.

isTesting: true conveys to AdMob that ads need to be shown for testing of the application. AdMob then keeps sending test ads to the application.

Let's get back to the steps.

6.   Navigate back to Project Explorer to open index.html (see Figure 9-20).

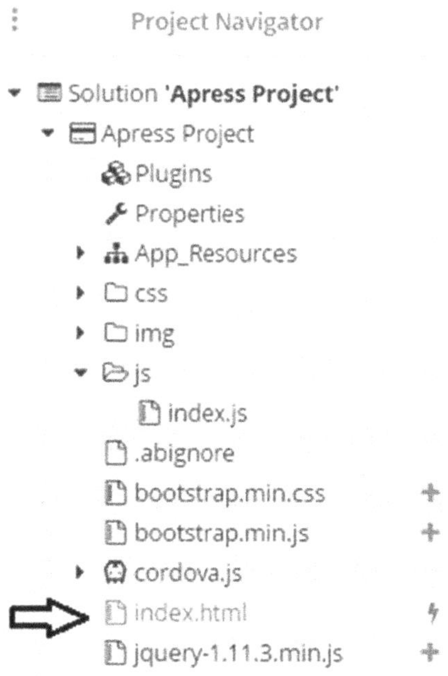

Project Navigator

▼ 🖻 Solution **'Apress Project'**
   ▼ 🗄 Apress Project
        🦖 Plugins
        🔧 Properties
     ▶ 🕸 App_Resources
     ▶ 🗀 css
     ▶ 🗀 img
     ▼ 🗁 js
         📄 index.js
       📄 .abignore
       📄 bootstrap.min.css   ✚
       📄 bootstrap.min.js   ✚
     ▶ 🌐 cordova.js
➡   📄 index.html   ⚡
       📄 jquery-1.11.3.min.js   ✚

Figure 9-20. *AppBuilder Project Explorer*

7. Open the index.html file for small modifications, such as the addition of code lines. The code lines mentioned and highlighted in Figure 9-21 make sure that Cordova and any plug-ins are loaded. The App.Initiate() line is responsible for loading of Cordova.js and plug-ins.

.

```
<body>
    <br /><br /><br />
    <div class="container">
        <div class="col-lg-3">
            Name: <input type="text" id="txtName" value="" />
        </div>
        <div class="col-lg-3">
            Address: <input type="text" id="txtAddress" value="" />
        </div>
        <div class="col-lg-3">
            <input type="button" id="btnCallServer" value="Call Server" />
        </div>
    </div>
    <div id="deviceready" class="blink">
            <p class="event listening">Connecting to Device</p>
            <p class="event received">Device is Ready</p>
    </div>
     <script type="text/javascript" src="cordova.js"></script>
     <script type="text/javascript" src="js/index.js"></script>
     <script type="text/javascript">
            app.initialize();
     </script>
</body>
</html>
```

Figure 9-21. *Project reference to Cordova file*

8. Save the contents.

9. Now, that almost everything is ready, click Run ➤ Build (see Figure 9-22).

175

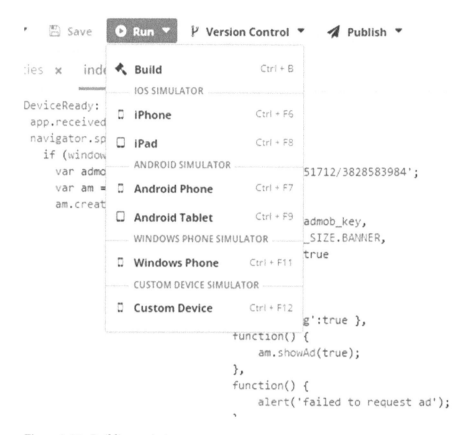

Figure 9-22. Building project

10.   On the next pop-up screen, select Android, and click Next (see Figure 9-23).

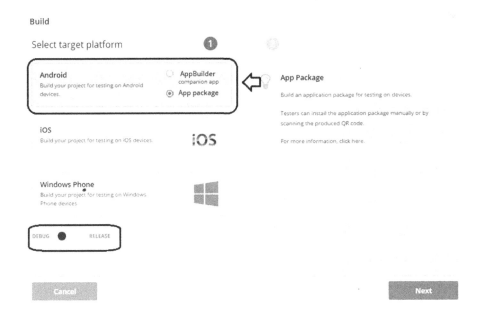

Figure 9-23. *Build process continued*

Make sure you compile the code in Debug mode because this is a trial account! Afterward, AppBuilder compiles the application and makes it available for download (see Figure 9-24).

Figure 9-24. *Build completed*

Now, download the Android-based APK file and install it. I have installed it on a Samsung Note 2 Android tablet. Being from unknown source, you may get a warning, but if allowed, everything goes smoothly.

The following are the installation steps.

    1.   Installation starts with a warning (see Figure 9-25).

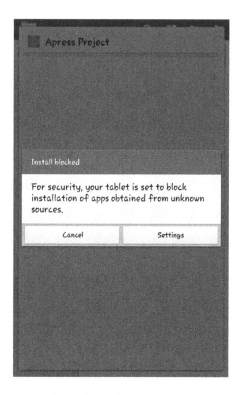

Figure 9-25. *App installation*

    2.   Installation continues after manually, allowing installation permission (see Figure 9-26).

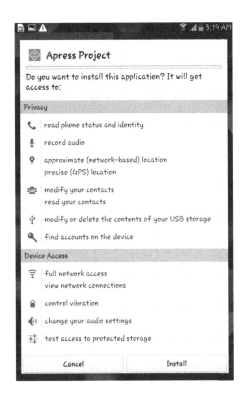

Figure 9-26. *App installation continued*

Figure 9-27 shows the installation in progress.

Figure 9-27. *App installation continued*

Figure 9-28 shows the installation completed.

Figure 9-28. App installation complete

3. Click Done.

4. Start the application. The Telerik logo is displayed because we are using the trial edition (see Figure 9-29). In the final version, it can be removed by navigating to Project Explorer.

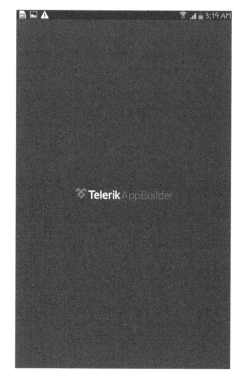

Figure 9-29. *App started*

Finally, the application with the test banner appears on the screen, as seen in Figure 9-30.

Figure 9-30. *App running with advertisement*

Isn't it easy to show ads? These ads are all for testing, which means you won't get paid by clicking these ads. Why? Remember that I mentioned isTesting: true in the index.js file earlier. For the final deployable version, make sure that isTesting is set to false. You can track earning from ads in the Monetize tab in the AdMob dashboard, as shown in Figure 9-31.

Figure 9-31. *AdMob dashboard*

You can also easily select ads through meditation as an AdMob option. Payments are made directly as per the terms mentioned when setting up an account. More information about payment criteria and terms are available at https://support.google.com/admob/checklist/2998383.

Let's make a note of the do's and don'ts while using ads in a project.

Don't

- Don't deploy an application on the test device with IsTesting false. When detected, an ad provider may block the account!

- Don't put ads in a location where it is banned! Respect each app provider's policies. For example, in Android, showing interstitial ads while the app is closing is against the ad policy. The solution is to try to place the ad between the navigation or as a banner ad.

Do

- Use an ad mediator, if possible.

- Pay close attention to deploying ads using iAd. iAd's policies are little complex compared to other providers.

Summary

This chapter covered how to integrate an ad framework into a hybrid application. You learned the basic differences between the various ad frameworks available in market.

The next chapter discusses working with third-party APIs.

CHAPTER 10

■ ■ ■

Working with Third-Party Services in HMAD

The objectives of this chapter are to

- Understand the various required services

- Understand how third-party components can help save time

- Learn about the costs and limitations of libraries

No matter which platform or framework that you choose for HMAD, there is always some functionality missing from the framework vendor. This gives third parties the chance to offer something and possibly make money out of it.

We have used Telerik AppBuilder throughout the book. All APIs required by a developer or project may not exist with AppBuilder, so AppBuilder has third-party plug-in integration. Some of the third-party plug-ins are also available for direct addition into the AppBuilder project properties.

This chapter discusses some of the popular plug-ins required by the project, such as the payment gateways and OpenID Authentication through Twitter or Facebook.

CAPTCHA APIs

We all know that CAPTCHA APIs are used by many web sites. It assures that a human is operating at the other end and not a robot! It works by asking complex questions in the form of images and sequences containing content like characters or numbers that are supposed to be identified. This can be done by humans only by manually reading the images' embedded contents.

There are also other forms of CAPTCHA API available on the market. Such forms may ask users to enter the characters or numbers emailed or sent over text message or a phone call. There is no direct plug-in that exists for CAPTCHA in AppBuilder-based HMAD.

So, you will have to REST or AJAX calls to achieve the same. One such third party can help with REST APIs.

Although a paid API, RingCaptcha has major benefits—it's easy to use, user-friendly, and has very powerful documentation. You can learn more about RingCaptcha at http://www.ringcaptcha.com.

You can refer a RingCaptcha–specific JS library into index.html, as shown in Figure 10-1.

```
<script type='text/javascript'
charset='UTF-8' src="//cdn.ringcaptcha.com/
widget/v2/bundle.min.js"/>
```

Figure 10-1. Refer RingCaptcha in the code

Instead of referring the JS file from the content delivery network (CDN), you can download and refer locally. The first step is to register at ringcaptcha.com. Then create an app at https://my.ringcaptcha.com/apps. You can get an app key and secret key. You can track the project by using the online dashboard at https://my.ringcaptcha.com/apps, as shown in Figure 10-2.

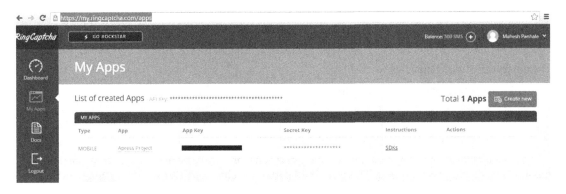

Figure 10-2. RingCaptcha portal

Further, you can use JavaScript or JQuery to call RingCaptcha to get updates regarding verification. JS code may look like this:

```
POST /${app_key}/code/${service} HTTP/1.1
Host: https://api.ringcaptcha.com
Content-Type: application/x-www-url-encoded, charset=utf-8
```

You can get an update in the callback, like this:

```
Status: 200 OK
{
    "id":"Transaction ID",
    "token":"Transaction token",
    "status":"SUCCESS or ERROR",
    "message":"Error code when Status is ERROR",
    "phone":"Cleansed phone number",
    "service":"Service used to send PIN code",
    "expires_in":"Seconds this token is still active",
    "retry_in":"Seconds you need to wait until a new request can be made"
}
```

The preceding code is referred from `https://my.ringcaptcha.com/docs/api`.

Refer to the URL mentioned earlier if you want to use this API over web, Android, and iPhone native applications.

OPEN ID Authentication

Nowadays, Internet users are never interested in creating a new user profile with a new username and password. Most Internet users have a Microsoft Live, Google, Yahoo!, Facebook, or Twitter account. So, instead of creating a new account on some web site or app, users prefer to use existing IDs so that they don't have to remember yet another username and password combo.

So, can we leverage the same Open ID Authentication in mobile apps as well? Yes! With AppBuilder, you can directly get an OAuth plug-in from the available and trusted plug-in set.

To use this plug-in, you have to first register at `https://oauth.io`. After all the registration formalities, you have to add integrated APIs. Over 120 OAuth providers can be used with the application including Twitter, Facebook, and so forth. A very detailed procedure on how to use such an API is offered by Telerik at `https://plug-ins.telerik.com/cordova/plug-in/oauth.io`. You can add many providers at the same time. An OAuth dashboard is shown in Figure 10-3.

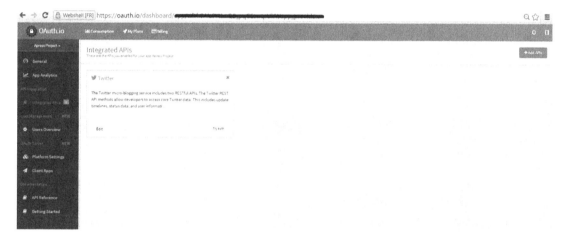

Figure 10-3. *OAuth.IO portal*

As you can see, I picked Twitter for the OAuth. The configuration panel is shown in Figure 10-4.

Figure 10-4. *OAuth.IO portal configuration*

As discussed earlier, we are required to have a public key (identifier number) passed. How do you get one? Refer to the next section, "Twitter API."

Twitter API

To create a Twitter account–based OAuth app, you must first have a Twitter account. As discussed earlier in the OAuth API (see Figure 10-4), you have to pass a public key and a secret key to make OAuth work.

So, create a Twitter account at `https://apps.twitter.com`, and then create an app. After all the formal details have been completed, you can find a public key and a secret key inside the dashboard (see Figure 10-5).

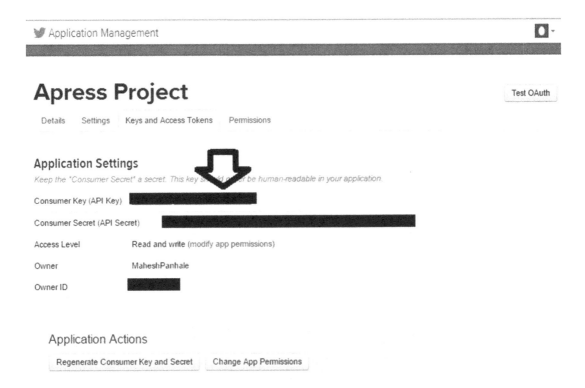

Figure 10-5. *Twitter integration*

After you get a public key and a secret key, pass it on to the OAuth API. To test connectivity between the OAuth API and Twitter, you can use the OAuth API's UI. Click the Test Auth button. The OAuth API should connect to Twitter. You may see the alert dialog shown in Figure 10-6.

Figure 10-6. *Twitter integration continued*

After this test, you can refer the following code (after installing OAuth plug-in) to integrate Twitter with the application.

```
OAuth.popup("twitter", {cache: true},function (result) {alert("Success: " + JSON.
stringify(result)),},function (err) {alert(err),}),
```

Other OAuth providers can be used in a similar way. One of the vital functionalities required nowadays is the ability to accept payments from the app user or client.

Payment Gateways

Many payment gateways exist. However, for mobile applications, many may prefer PayPal or Paytm. A plug-in for PayPal can be loaded directly from Telerik trusted plug-ins (see Figure 10-7).

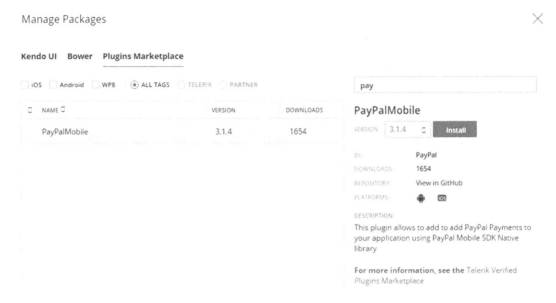

Figure 10-7. *PayPal integration*

A very good, easy, step-by-step example is on GitHub at `https://github.com/Telerik-Verified-Plug-ins/PayPal`.

You may be required to have a PayPal account. To use the account, you have to provide valid bank information. This verification is normally done by transferring a random amount of money, like $0.77 to the account. You are asked about this amount during verification. After creating a PayPal account, you get two client ids: for production and for testing.

The following code can be referred to integrate with the PayPal with application.

```
var clientIDs =
  {
     "PayPalEnvironmentProduction": "YOUR_PRODUCTION_CLIENT_ID",
     "PayPalEnvironmentSandbox": "YOUR_SANDBOX_CLIENT_ID"
  },
  PayPalMobile.init(clientIDs, app.onPayPalMobileInit),
```

GPS Services

We used an HTML5 API in previous chapters to track location. Paid services can also be purchased, in terms of REST APIs from providers like HERE Maps.

Summary

In this chapter, you learned about the various plug-ins available for Captcha, payment gateways, and Open ID Authentication. Increasingly, you can find more plug-ins from vendors. PhoneGap is a vendor that is rich with plug-ins.

The next chapter discusses the set up and deployment of HMAD.

CHAPTER 11

Setup and Deployment

Objectives of this chapter:

- Understand license costs of HMAD
- Learn the procedures to follow during deployment
- Understand the pros and cons of deploying to each platform

This chapter presents the setup and deployment procedures required to get an application on a device. These procedures may require purchasing a license from certain companies or vendors. This chapter will help you understand the basic costs required to create an application.

Obtaining Vendor-Specific Developer Licenses

Normally, before deployment, the only cost was for an AppBuilder or Telerik license, or for whichever hybrid mobile development platform you picked up.

Today, the cost for a developer license is as follows:

- *Google*: $25, payable one time
- *Apple*: $99 per year
- *Microsoft*: $19 per year (individual) or $99 per year (company)

These prices are in effect at the time of this writing, but may vary in the future.

Let's explore the publishing process for Apple's App Store now.

Deploying to the Apple App Store

After developing and testing an application (which could be done in a simulator), you can publish the application on Apple App Store. To do so using AppBuilder, the following prerequisites exist:

- Make sure your project is open in AppBuilder.
- Make sure you have a valid cryptographic certificate containing your identity, which in turn can be used to create a publisher profile. The publisher profile further contains your app ID and may optionally contain a list of registered devices on which you can install your application.
- If you already have a provisioning profile created, you can import it from the first tab before CryptoGraphic Identities.

Figure 11-1 shows how to open a certificate and profile import window.

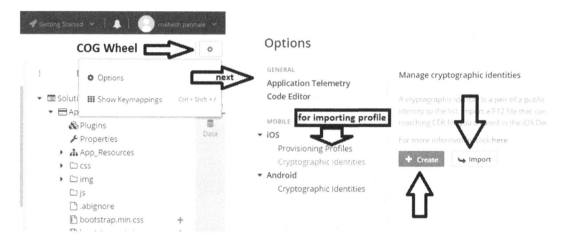

Figure 11-1. *AppBuilder configuration for Apple device-based application*

To publish your app, follow these steps:

1. After your profile import or creation, click Publish ä App Store, as shown in Figure 11-2. (Keep in mind that the steps after this do not work with a trial edition of AppBuilder.)

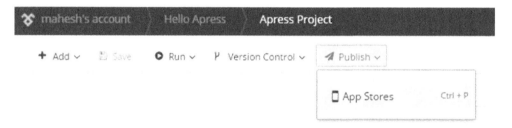

Figure 11-2. *Publishing your app on App Store*

2. After selecting an App Store, you choose a profile (which you've already imported in the previous steps).

3. Click Download to download the application package and upload it manually in iTunes Connect. You need an OS X system to complete this task.

4. You may optionally use AppBuilder to help you publish the application, but you will have to submit your Apple ID and password.

5. If the Apple ID exceeds 40 characters, you will have to publish the app manually using the OS X system. That process is outlined in the remaining steps. First, visit and log in to `https://itunesconnect.apple.com/`.

6. Click Manage Your Apps.

7. Click the Add New App option. Select iOS App, and fill out the App information form.

8. In the next screen, fill in the details about price and the application's availability.

9. Enter metadata (more information) about your application in subsequent dialog boxes.

10. Upload the final output received from AppBuilder (the app file).

11. Click Save and then Submit for Review.

The review process at Apple's end may take more time than the process for Android or Windows Phone. After approval, your app can be seen in the App Store.

More details about using AppBuilder to upload your iOS app to the App Store can be found here: http://docs.telerik.com/platform/appbuilder/publishing-your-app/distribute-production/publish-ios.

Deploying to Google Play

Once the development and testing of your application (which could be done on a simulator) is complete, you can publish the app on Google Play. To do so using AppBuilder, the following prerequisites exist:

- Make sure your project is open in AppBuilder.

- Make sure you have built the project in release mode.

- Download the APK file as you did in Chapter 4.

- Make sure you have an account with Google and have paid the one-time fee of $25.

To publish your app, follow these steps:

1. Visit and log in to https://play.google.com/apps/publish/.

2. Click Add New Application in the top-right corner. The window shown in Figure 11-3 appears.

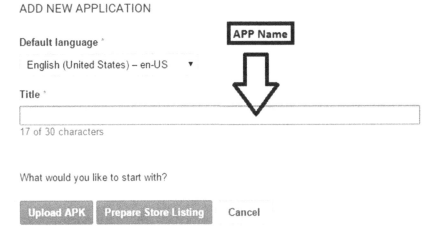

Figure 11-3. *Google Play—uploading a new app*

3. Give your app a title. Click the Upload APK button. Browse to the APK file and upload.

4. Click Store Listing to provide a description of your app, as shown in Figure 11-4.

Figure 11-4. *Google Play—configuring the app*

5. On the Content Rating tab, you can set your app's content rating.

6. The next important step is to set up pricing and distribution. Click the Pricing & Distribution tab and set price details, as shown in Figure 11-5.

Figure 11-5. *Google Play—setting the app's price*

7. After all information is added, click Submit.

   Your app will be reviewed and made available on Google Play, typically within seven to eight hours of submission.

Deploying to Windows Store

Once the development and testing of your application (which may be done on a simulator) is complete, you can publish it on Windows Store. To do so using AppBuilder, the following prerequisites exist:

- Make sure your project is open in AppBuilder.

- Make sure you have built the project in release mode.

- Make sure you have a Windows Dev Center account.

To publish your app, follow these steps:

1. In the App Builder, click Publish (just as you did for iOS publishing).

2. Select the Windows Phone Store option.

3. Click the Build option.

4. Download the output XAP on your local machine.

5. Log in to `http://dev.windowsphone.com/en-us`.

6. Complete the submission process as detailed at `https://dev.windows.com/en-us/publish`.

After the submission is complete, the app will be reviewed by Microsoft. If everything goes well, your app may get approval within a few hours of submission.

Understanding the Pros and Cons

You might not find Windows Phone and Android deployment difficult. However, because of UI norms at Apple, about 30 percent of submitted applications get rejected, according to VentureBeat.

One thing to understand is that your app is tested on actual devices when it comes to Apple and Microsoft.

The app certification process is quicker nowadays, compared to the past, when it used to take 7-15 days.

Android APK files can be distributed directly as well by using via BlueTooth or Wi-Fi. However, for Apple and Windows, direct installation for the APP or XAP file is not allowed unless you have a phone with a test account for the respective vendors.

Tracing and Logging

Developers can keep track of their apps by viewing details about app sales, profit and loss, and user visits indicated by geography. Such details can be seen on online dashboards provided by the respective vendors, including Microsoft, Apple, and Google.

Summary

This chapter explained the costs of hybrid mobile application development for the three main platforms. The chapter also presented the steps to follow for deploying applications. You can go through manual submission or use AppBuilder.

The next chapter covers another hybrid mobile application development platform: Xamarin.

■ ■ ■

XAMARIN vs. HMAD

Objectives of this chapter:

- Learn about managed applications

- Understand how Xamarin works

- Understand the pros and cons of using Xamarin

- Compare Xamarin with HMAD

Xamarin is an interesting platform for mobile application development. The motive behind Xamarin is the same as that of hybrid mobile applications! Just as you define HTML5-based hybrid applications and after packaging deploy them on various platforms, Xamarin does a similar thing.

The basic difference is that with Xamarin, you code in C#.

Introduction to Managed Applications

Do you know the .NET or Mono .NET Framework? Have you ever coded in C#? Do you know the basics of XAML? Do you want to develop mobile applications that target multiple platforms?

If the answer to all these questions is yes, Xamarin is the platform for you! The Xamarin platform leverages the expertise of the C# language for business logic and XAML for the UI.

What is XAML? *Extensible Application Markup Language* (XAML) was introduced by Microsoft along with the Windows Presentation Foundation (WPF) framework around 10 years back. It is based on a container-content control relationship: each control can act as a container and can contain another control as content. Thus it makes 2D and 3D vector-based (with a z axis) UIs possible.

Using WPF, you can define a Windows OS–based desktop application with easy complex UI creation! Figures 12-1, 12-2, and 12-3 show the XAML UI, code, and output, respectively, for a simple WPF program.

```xml
<Window x:Class="WpfApplication1.MainWindow"
        xmlns="http://schemas.microsoft.com/winfx/2006/xaml/presentation"
        xmlns:x="http://schemas.microsoft.com/winfx/2006/xaml"
        Title="MainWindow" Height="300" Width="300">
    <StackPanel>
        <Button Height="200" Width="200" Click="OnCLICK">
            <Button.Content>
                <MediaElement Source="C:\Test.wmv" Height="100" Width="100"
                              Name="myvideo" LoadedBehavior="Manual" />
            </Button.Content>
        </Button>
    </StackPanel>
</Window>
```

WPF UI FILE WITH .XAML EXTENSION

Figure 12-1. *XAML UI*

```csharp
public partial class MainWindow : Window
{
    public MainWindow()
    {
        InitializeComponent();
    }

    private void OnCLICK(object sender, RoutedEventArgs e)
    {
        myvideo.Play();
    }
}
```

WPF Code File with .CS Extension

Figure 12-2. *XAML code-behind in C#*

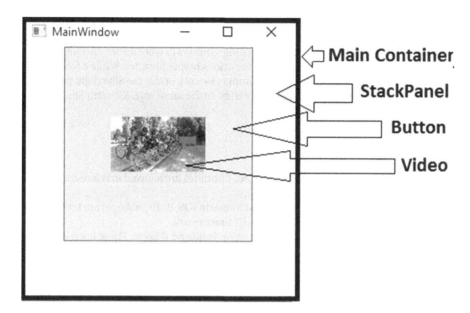

Figure 12-3. *WPF code output*

Similar XAML, with minute changes, can be used for developing Silverlight and Windows Phone applications. Silverlight is a Flash-like framework. Applications created using Silverlight work as in-browser or browser-based" applications. Making these applications work requires a plug-in or player installation as an extension on top of the browser.

How Does Xamarin Work?

Just like Java for Android and Objective C for iPhone, C# on .NET has been a development language and platform for Windows Phone development since the beginning. What is different with Xamarin is that it makes XAML and C# code work on iPhone and Android. In this section, you'll learn how the XAML- and C#-based code work on different platforms. Let's take a look at them one by one.

Using Xamarin for Windows Phone

Since C# and XAML are natively preferred by Windows Phone, you really don't require Xamarin tools for Windows Phone applications. However, using Xamarin Studio for development makes it easy to write reusable code that can later be used for iPhone and Android development.

For Windows Phone, C# code is compiled into Microsoft Intermediate Language (MSIL). Later it is executed by the built-in runtime on Windows Phone.

It's interesting to see how code works on Android and iPhone. The Microsoft .NET Framework provides many helper libraries. Such libraries are normally called Framework Class Libraries (FCLs). These libraries include helper classes to deal with the database, filesystem, network, security, and so on. References to such helper libraries are required when you start coding desktop or web-based applications using .NET. While working with Silverlight applications, certain limitations exist. For example, references to the database helper library are not allowed in Silverlight for security reasons.

To help programmers know which libraries are allowed and which are not allowed in a specific type of application, an editor such as Microsoft Visual Studio works on the concept of a framework profile. While a normal application is under development, Visual Studio allows programmers to work under the Full .NET Framework profile, which in turn allows programmers to refer to various helper libraries. While a Silverlight application is under development, Visual Studio allows programmers to work under the Silverlight profile, which in turn allows programmers to refer to specific helper libraries. In the same way, Xamarin Studio also works on the profile concept.

Using Xamarin for Android

Xamarin Studio uses a Xamarin Mobile profile, which specific .NET libraries are allowed to reference, irrespective of the targeted vendor (such as Android or iPhone).

Xamarin offers two profile products: Xamarin.Android and Xamarin.iOS. Both packages are built on top of the Mono .NET Framework, an open source version of the .NET Framework.

Two libraries are offered by Xamarin in order to code against Android and iPhone. These libraries include `Mono.Android.dll` for Android and `MonoTouch.dll` for iPhone. Full lists of libraries for Android and iPhone are available at the following sites:

- `https://developer.xamarin.com/guides/ios/under_the_hood/assemblies/`

- `https://developer.xamarin.com/guides/android/under_the_hood/assemblies/`

The Xamarin platform also helps programmers compile code and deliver mobile-platform-specific output such as APK for Android and APP for iPhone.

Figure 12-4 depicts the Xamarin architecture.

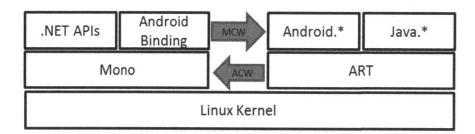

Figure 12-4. *Xamarin working on Android*

Xamarin-based Android applications execute on the Mono Runtime, which in turn executes parallel to the Android Runtime (ART). Both are based on the Linux kernel. Functionalities provided by the Android Runtime can be referred to in the Xamarin program by using .NET through an Android Callable Wrapper (ACW). ACW ultimately acts like a bridge between Java native APIs for Android and .NET.

If you want to override the native Java implementation using .NET code, you can use the Managed Callable Wrapper (MCW) given by the Xamarin .NET APIs.

Using Xamarin for iPhone

Xamarin has an ahead-of-time (AOT) compiler that compiles Xamarin-based iOS applications into assembly code. Because the UI is a major concern for iPhone applications, Xamarin offers the Cocoa Touch SDK from Apple through wrappers in C#. Wrapper APIs make it easy for .NET developers to refer to Cocoa APIs without understanding their complexity.

To facilitate the development, testing, and publishing of iPhone applications, Xamarin also offers Xamarin Studio on iOS or Mac as well.

In all the platforms, Xamarin applications can leverage the existing runtime without worrying about handling memory allocation or garbage collection, as the Mono Framework–based runtime handles it implicitly.

How much does Xamarin cost? At the time of writing this book, the Xamarin cost for an individual is $25 per month. For businesses and enterprises, the cost varies from $999 to $1,899 per year.

Exploring Xamarin Features

Xamarin has special features, including the following:

- It has libraries that are wrapper libraries around the entire Android and iPhone SDKs.

- It provides wrapper libraries around the Objective C, Java, C, and C++ APIs.

- You can use core .NET features along with wrappers, including Language Integrated Query (LINQ) and parallel programming.

- The IDE used for development is either Xamarin Studio or Visual Studio.

- Xamarin Studio is also available on the Mac OS.

- About 90 percent of the code can be shared across the platforms, according to Xamarin.com.

Xamarin vs. HMAD

When compared with hybrid application development using HTML5, Xamarin also has limitations. Table 12-1 compares HMAD and Xamarin development.

Table 12-1. Hybrid Applications: Xamarin-Based Development vs. HTML5-Based Development

Platforms / Points	Hybrid Mobile Application Development Using HTML5	Xamarin Development
Language	JavaScript/JS libraries such as jQuery.	C#.
UI challenges	UI development uses HTML5.	UI uses XAML only.
Code reusability	When used with a framework or platform such as AppBuilder, the UI and code are almost reusable.	UI code is not sharable because of the norms on iPhone.
App size	Small compared to Xamarin.	Larger, because of the libraries being packaged into the application.

(*continued*)

Table 12-1. (*continued*)

Platforms / Points	Hybrid Mobile Application Development Using HTML5	Xamarin Development
Availability of resources	More resources in terms of man-hours are available from a web background.	Fewer resources are available on the market.
Learning curve	For a developer familiar with the Web, the learning curve is less.	XAML learning is little complex compared to HTML!
Miscellaneous	You can use various platforms and editors for code, including PhoneGap, AppBuilder, and Ionic.	Only Xamarin/Visual Studio are available.
	Resource cleaning and memory cleaning is the job of the programmer and needs to be achieved through code only.	Resource cleaning or memory cleaning is a job of the platform runtime.
	Cost differs widely from packaging platform to platform.	Cost is on the higher side when it comes to full Xamarin Studio.

Summary

So what is good for you, as a developer: Xamarin or HTML5-based HMAD? Again you get the consultant's answer: it depends! Now that you know about Xamarin, how it works, what it costs, and the editors available, you could easily find Xamarin attractive. To make your decision, you have to consider the following:

- Functionality required

- Resources available and their expertise

- Cost

Finally, to conclude: no platform is bad, and each has its own benefits.

■ ■ ■

Case Study: A Practical Approach

Your most unhappy customers are your greatest source of learning.

—Bill Gates

The preceding quotation tells the gist of our first case study. How do you identify what a client feels about your product or service? Can you digitize the process? Can you make the feedback data-collection process easy? Can you make an app for that? The answer to these questions is definitely yes.

This case study, presented courtesy of SEED Management Services, targets services offered at any hotel SEED Management Services is a company based in Pune, India that has developed an app called Survey Data ++. This app handles digitization of long and complex questionnaires.

This chapter covers the steps to be taken to complete the application.

The prerequisites for this process are as follows:

- Make sure you have set up an AppBuilder account at www.telerik.com.

- Make sure you have read the previous chapters to understand the concepts behind hybrid mobile application development.

- Download jquery-1.10.2.js from www.JQuery.com.

- Download the Star Rating plug-in from www.krajee.com.

- Make sure that along with the Star Rating jQuery plug-in, you have the star-rating. css file.

- Download bootstrap-3.0 CSS files from http://getbootstrap.com/ for a responsive UI.

Creating a Feedback Application

Let's get started with the application:

1. Log in to https://platform.telerik.com/#workspaces, as shown in Figure 13-1.

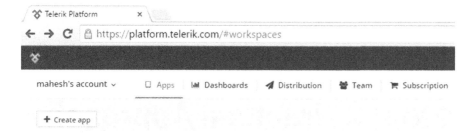

Figure 13-1. *AppBuilder—creating a workspace*

2. Click the Create App button.

3. Fill in all the details on the next screen, as shown in Figure 13-2.

Figure 13-2. *AppBuilder—continuing to create a project*

4. Click the Create App button.

5. On the next screen, shown in Figure 13-3, click the Create AppBuilder Hybrid Project button.

Figure 13-3. *AppBuilder—project creation continued*

6. The screen shown in Figure 13-4 appears. Enter details as shown and then click Create Project.

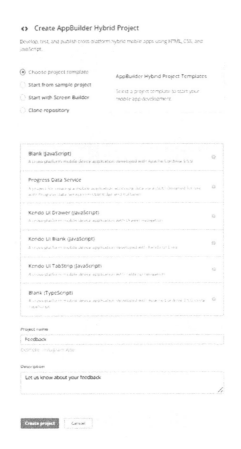

Figure 13-4. *AppBuilder—project creation continued*

7. A project workspace—the default Project Navigator window—appears, as shown in Figure 13-5.

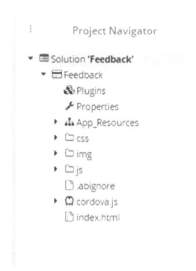

Figure 13-5. *AppBuilder—Project Navigator*

8. Add the files indicated in the list of prerequisites earlier. Figure 13-6 shows the project structure after adding the files.

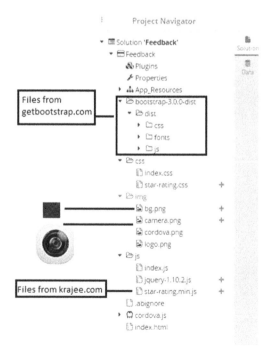

Figure 13-6. *AppBuilder—displaying the project content*

9. Open index.html from the Project Navigator.

10. Let's inject code into index.html. Import the required JavaScript and CSS files into the <head> tag, as shown in Figure 13-7.

```
<script src="js/jquery-1.10.2.js"></script>
<link href="bootstrap-3.0.0-dist/dist/css/bootstrap.min.css" rel="stylesheet" />
<link href="bootstrap-3.0.0-dist/dist/css/bootstrap-theme.min..css" rel="stylesheet" />
<link href="css/star-rating.css" rel="stylesheet" type="text/css" />
```

Figure 13-7. AppBuilder—index.html references

11. Add a <title> for the page and a required style for the message and content divs, as shown in Figure 13-8.

```
<title>Yummy! Feedback</title>

<style>
    #dvcontent { max-width:750px;margin:0 auto; }
    header { margin:0 auto; }
    body,#dvcontent,#dvthankyou
    {
        font-family: 'Droid Sans', sans-serif;
        background-image:url(img/bg.png);
    }
</style>
```

Figure 13-8. Title and style markup code

The <body> content at a glance will look like Figure 13-9.

```
<body>
    <div id="dvcontent" class="container">...</div>

    <div id="dvthankyou">...</div>

    <script type="text/javascript" src="cordova.js"></script>
    <script src="bootstrap-3.0.0-dist/dist/js/bootstrap.min.js"></script>
    <script id="starRating" src="js/star-rating.min.js" type="text/javascript"></script>

    <script>...</script>

</body>
```

Figure 13-9. HTML UI—markup code

The main `<div>` container contents are a hotel label, camera icon, and feedback form, as shown in Figure 13-10.

```
<div id="dvcontent" class="container">

    <span class="col-lg-6" style="font-weight:bold;font-size:75px;color:white;">Yummy !</span>

    <span class="col-lg-6">
        <img id="userimg" src="img/camera.png" class="img-thumbnail" width="100" height="100" style="float:right">
    </span>

    <hr style="color:white;">

    <table id="tblcontent" class="table table-bordered table-responsive">...</table>

</div>
```

Figure 13-10. *Responsive containers in the markup*

The feedback form is a responsive `<table>`. Note that the text boxes used in `<table>` are with specific classes referenced from the Star Rating jQuery plug-in. The rest of the classes used are from responsive CSS and are discussed in Chapter 7. See Figure 13-11.

```
<table id="tblcontent" class="table table-bordered table-responsive">

    <tr>
        <td>
            <label class="label label-default">Food :</label>
        </td>
        <td><input id="txtrate" value=0 type=number class=rating  data-default-caption={rating}  max=" 5" step="1 " data-size=sm data-stars="5"></td>
    </tr>

    <tr>
        <td>
            <label class="label label-default"> Service :</label>
        </td>
        <td><input id="txtservice" value=0 type=number class=rating  data-default-caption={rating}  max=" 5" step="1 " data-size=sm data-stars="5"></td>
    </tr>

    <tr>
        <td>
            <label class="label label-default"> Comment :</label>
        </td>
        <td>
            <textarea id="txtcomment" cols="15" rows="3" class="form-control"></textarea>
        </td>
    </tr>

    <tr>
        <td colspan="2">
            <button id="btnsubmit" class="btn btn-lg btn-primary btn-block">Submit</button>
        </td>
    </tr>

</table>
```

Figure 13-11. *Responsive containers in markup continued*

The next `<div>` is for displaying a Thank You message to the customer, as shown in Figure 13-12. This step completes the UI.

```
<div id="dvthankyou" style="display:none;color:white;">
    <h1>
        Thank you for your valuable feedback!
    </h1>
</div>
```

Figure 13-12. A div container for the message

Writing the Business Logic

Now let's focus on jQuery code. Follow these steps:

1. The code snippet in Figure 13-13 does the validation and collects data entered by the customer in the feedback form via the Submit button click. Copy this code and paste it into the `<script>` ...`</script>` block inside the `index.html` page:

```
$('#btnsubmit').click(function () {
    if ($('#txtrate').val() == 0) {
        alert('Please rate food');
    }
    else if ($('#txtservice').val() == 0) {
        alert('Please rate service(s)');
    }
    else if ($.trim($('#txtcomment').val()) == "") {
        alert('Please comment!');
    }
    else {
        //store in JSON
        ansJSON['foodrate'] = $('#txtrate').val();
        ansJSON['servicerate'] = $('#txtservice').val();
        ansJSON['comment'] = $('#txtcomment').val();
        ansJSON['imagestring'] = $('#userimg').attr('src');

        //Write in SDCARD
        document.addEventListener("deviceready", onDeviceReady, false);
    }
});
```

Figure 13-13. Validation and data collection using jQuery code

2. The code shown in Figure 13-14 captures an image from the camera with a JPEG extension. Copy and paste this code as a continuation to the preceding block, between the `<script>` `</script>` tags inside the `index.html` page.

```
//get picture using camera
$('#userimg').click(function () {
    pictureSource = navigator.camera.PictureSourceType;
    destinationType = navigator.camera.DestinationType;
    capturePhoto();
});

function capturePhoto() {
    // Take picture using device camera and retrieve image as base64-encoded string
    navigator.camera.getPicture(onPhotoDataSuccess, onFail, {
        quality: 50,
        destinationType: Camera.DestinationType.DATA_URL,
        sourceType: Camera.PictureSourceType.CAMERA,
        encodingType: Camera.EncodingType.JPEG,
        targetWidth: 500,
        targetHeight: 500,
        correctOrientation: true,
        saveToPhotoAlbum: false
    });
}
```

Figure 13-14. *Camera picture-collection code using jQuery*

3.   Figure 13-15 shows the supporting functions for storing feedback data and the photo image. These functions are discussed in Chapter 8. This step completes the entire code.

```
//write file to SDcard
function OnDeviceReady() {
    window.requestFileSystem(LocalFileSystem.PERSISTENT, 0, FoundFS, OnFailure);
}

function FoundFS(fileSystem) {
    fname = "Feedbacksurvey-" + device.uuid + ".json"; //create filename
    fileSystem.root.getFile(fname, { create: true, exclusive: false }, FoundFileEntry, OnFailure);
}

function FoundFileEntry(fileEntry) {
    fileEntry.createWriter(FoundFileWriter, OnFailure);
}

function FoundFileWriter(writer) {
    writer.write(JSON.stringify(ansJSON));
    ansJSON = {};
    $('#tblcontent').hide();
    $('#dvthankyou').show();
    alert('File Stored Successfully..');
}

function OnFailure(error) {
    alert(error.code);
}
```

```
// Called when a photo is successfully retrieved
function onPhotoDataSuccess(imageData) {
    var smallImage = document.getElementById("userimg");
    smallImage.style.display = 'block';

    // Show the captured photo
    smallImage.src = "data:image/jpeg;base64," + imageData;
    $('#userimg').css('width', '100px');
    $('#userimg').css('height', '100px');
}

// Called if something bad happens.
function onFail(message) {
    alert('Failed because: ' + message);
}
```

Figure 13-15. *Photo and data access functions using jQuery/ JavaScript*

4. Now, do the build as shown in Figure 13-16. We already discussed the build process in Chapter 4.

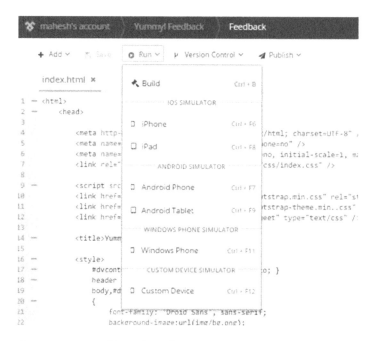

Figure 13-16. Build ing the code

5. Do the package building as discussed in Chapter 4.

6. Install and test the application on the respective devices.

   Figure 13-17 shows snapshots of the application from the device and simulators.

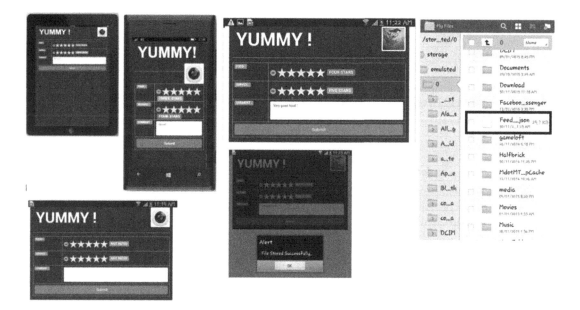

Figure 13-17. application, under execution on different devices

Summary

In this chapter, you created a feedback system application as a hybrid mobile application. You used camera access and file storage within the device's SD card itself. The case study illustrated that JSON and jQuery AJAX are vital for developing hybrid mobile applications.

Index

P, Q

PhoneGap, 49

R

Representational State Transfer (REST), 48
Research In Motion Limited (RIM), 3
Responsive CSS, 48

S

Sencha Touch, 51
Server-side support, 46
Service-oriented architecture (SOA), 8, 61
    CSS, 48
    REST, 48
    Skeleton, 48
    Twitter Bootstrap, 48
    WCF services, 47
    web services, 46–47
Shockwave Flash, 30
Silverlight, 30
Skeleton, 48

T

Third-party services
    CAPTCHA APIs
        JS code, 186
        portal code, 186–187
        RingCaptcha, 186
        web sites, 185
    GPS services, 191
    OAuth (see OPEN ID authentication)
    objectives, 185
    payment gateways
        PayPal integration, 190
        programming code, 191
Touch Punch, 138
Twitter API
    application code, 190
    integration, 188
Twitter Bootstrap, 48

U

User interface (UI)
    event handling
        bind () function, 134
        browser, 135

        click () function, 134
        dynamic UI generation, 135
        JQuery plug-in-based approach, 136–137
        on () function, 134
    HTML/JQuery
        controls/handling events, 129
        dynamic UI, 129
        dynamic UI building, 133
        HelloServer project, 130
        index.html, 132
        integer type, 130
        JSON output, 132
        SayHello.ashx, 129, 131
    miscellaneous libraries and plugins
        fusion chart, 137
        Touch Punch, 138
    objectives, 129
    responsive UI
        libraries/CSS frameworks, 138
        Skeleton, 138
        style classes, 138
        Twitter Bootstrap, 138

V

Vendor-specific developer licenses, HMAD, 193

W

Web applications vs. Hybrid
        mobile applications, 35–36
Windows Communication
        Foundation (WCF) services, 47
Windows Phone, 89
    layers, 29
Windows Store, HMAD, 197
Wireless Application Protocol (WAP), 2
Worldwide Developers
        Conference (WWDC) 12, 2015
World Wide Web Consortium (W3C), 29

X, Y, Z

Xamarin, 199
    for Android, 202
    vs. HMAD, 203
    for iPhone, 202
    special features, 203
    for Windows Phone, 201
XML, 41–42
XMLHttpRequest (XHR), 42

Get the eBook for only $5!

Why limit yourself?

Now you can take the weightless companion with you wherever you go and access your content on your PC, phone, tablet, or reader.

Since you've purchased this print book, we're happy to offer you the eBook in all 3 formats for just $5.

Convenient and fully searchable, the PDF version enables you to easily find and copy code—or perform examples by quickly toggling between instructions and applications. The MOBI format is ideal for your Kindle, while the ePUB can be utilized on a variety of mobile devices.

To learn more, go to www.apress.com/companion or contact support@apress.com.

Apress®
THE EXPERT'S VOICE™

Printed in the United States
By Bookmasters